William Carlos Williams

The Knack of Survival in America

Robert Coles

William Carlos Williams
The Knack of Survival in America

MASON WELCH GROSS LECTURESHIP SERIES

 RUTGERS UNIVERSITY PRESS
New Brunswick   New Jersey

Library of Congress Cataloging in Publication Data

Coles, Robert.
    William Carlos Williams: the knack of survival in America.

    (Mason Welch Gross lectureship series)
    Includes bibliographical references.
    1. Williams, William Carlos, 1883–1963 – Prose.
I. Series.
PS3545.I544Z583   813'.5'2   75-6560
ISBN 0-8135-0800-2

The Stecher Trilogy—*White Mule, In the Money,* and *The Build-up*—as well as *The Farmer's Daughters* (short stories), *Imaginations* (collected early prose), *In the American Grain* (essays), and *A Voyage to Pagany* are published by New Directions and can be ordered through their distributor, J. B. Lippincott Co., East Washington Square, Philadelphia, Pa. 19105.

To Jane, and to our sons,
Bob, Dan, and Mike

Contents

Introduction

This book came about because I was asked to give the annual Mason Gross Lectures at Rutgers University in 1974. But I have been thinking about some of the issues that come up in the following pages for many years, because the poor and working-class families I have worked with are not unlike the men, women, and children William Carlos Williams brings to life so dramatically and thoughtfully in the short stories and novels I choose to discuss here. Long before I wrote the Mason Gross Lectures I started suggesting a reading of some of Dr. Williams' stories to some of the youths I know who live in what I suppose sociologists would call "street-car suburbs," towns or sections of Boston not all that far from the so-called "inner city"; and it has been extraordinarily helpful for me to hear the responses—frank, pointed, insistent comments from young men and women who have never gone to college, who work in factories or stores or offices, who struggle hard to get by, but who share with the people Dr. Williams treated and watched so closely moral dilemmas perhaps best summarized by, of all people, Sören Kierkegaard: "How do I live a life?"

The Danish theologian asked that question in the course of taking to task Hegel, the philosopher who aimed unashamedly to come up with an answer, a formulation, an analysis, a prognostication, a theory to fit everyone and take care of everything — except for one matter: how does one get along from day to day, thread one's way through the ambiguities and obstacles and hardships of "plain, ordinary life," to use a phrase English essayists and novelists of the nineteenth century used without prejudice. Dr. Williams made no effort to conceal his attitude toward all too many self-important intellectuals; he was himself a broadly educated and introspective man, not only a poet but the social historian who came forth with a minor but unique masterpiece, *In the American Grain.* Yet, he worried about pedants, those who would take the poems, stories, novels he or others wrote and render them inert, lifeless, the stuff of academic abstraction — or to him just as bad, the foils for various kinds of ideological warfare. In the stories that make up *Life Along the Passaic River* and in his trilogy devoted to the rise of the immigrants Gurlie and Joe Stecher (*White Mule, In the Money* and *The Build-Up*), one feels him not only trying hard with his prose to contrive plots, develop believable and interesting characters, keep our interest in the dramatic action he presents, portray a whole range of social habits and customs, but also contend strenuously with those who want, above all, and at any cost, it seems, to strip men and women of their particularity, and maybe, too, the complexity of their lives, the moral ambiguities they have to face and not always banish, the ironies and contradictions which plague them, no matter how "simple" their life.

Above all, as he himself kept saying, Williams could not stop wondering what it means to be an ordinary American citizen—a factory worker, an office worker, a shop-keeper, a "laborer." Nor was he one to ruminate in the abstract; he was a physician whose life harnessed him to the utterly concrete: this child or parent who arrives in the office with a specific complaint. He would complain bitterly about his medical work; at least when he was trying to write he did: less time for the words. But he was, really, never interested in becoming a different person. He snatched time from his medical practice to write, yes; but he left his typewriter because for him there was no other choice. Certainly his stories and novels are inconceivable without the frame of mind years of clinical practice brought to him. One doesn't have to be a physician to write first-rate novels and stories, but the man who wrote *Life Along the Passaic River* and the Stecher trilogy wrote with a doctor's eye for children and for the suffering poor; and, of course, the stories for the most part are obviously autobiographical, even as a pediatrician appears in the Stecher trilogy to speak his mind about children and their parents.

Having spelled out the occasion for this book, I ought to add that when I was an undergraduate, I was very much interested in Dr. Williams' poetry; at that time I wrote a long critical essay on *Paterson.* And when I was in medical school, I met him and corresponded with him. I especially remember an afternoon in 1954, when I had begun an internship and he had come to a nearby university to read his poems. He already had suffered a stroke; it was painful for him to get some of his own words out, but he did, and with dignity and power. Afterwards a number of us had a chance to meet him and he and I talked at some length about his prose — especially the stories in *Life Along the Passaic* and the Stecher trilogy. I had long been taken with both, but the further along my medical education advanced, the more appreciative I became — and not only because Dr. Williams was a doctor who wrote, or a writer who maintained an active medical practice; quite simply, he knew how to tell compelling stories about the people whose lives he wanted to describe — knew how to put in words the language

they used with each other, the comedies and trag-
edies they were heir to, the unspoken daydreams
they had, the nightmares they experienced; in
Flannery O'Connor's words, "the mystery and
manners" of ordinary life. When I told Dr. Williams
that someday, somehow, I would like to register an
approving nod to those two efforts (the trilogy I
regard as one sustained fictional narrative), he said
he hoped I would, not because he wanted specific
scrutiny of his own writing, but because by then
few people were paying much attention to either
people like those in the Passaic stories or to people
like the Stechers. He added: "I mean novelists are
ignoring them; the sociologists and psychologists
have taken over. At least someone cares."

That was exactly twenty years ago. In the interim,
the social scientists he referred to have continued
their studies, sometimes to valuable effect (I think
of the work of Herbert Gans or Richard Sennett)
but sometimes in a manner that makes one cry
loud and sadly for a novelist of Williams' talent,
sensibility, and experience to come, please come
and help straighten things out—rescue us from
sweeping generalizations, from a myriad of statistics,
from moralistic judgments concealed as factual
assertion, and, worst of all, from the heavy, murky
jargon we have had to grow used to. Over the years,
as I have watched, for instance, young activists at
work in our urban ghettoes or among the rural

poor, and heard them talk about so-and-so's "theory," or the latest bit of mumbo-jumbo to come out
of someone else's "research design," all supposedly
meant to "explain" something called the "socio-
cultural" (or is it "psycho-social"?) "behavior" of
this or that "population group," I have thought of
the doctor who figures in the Passaic stories, or for
that matter, of Gurlie Stecher: both of them did
not suffer fools gladly. So, when there was a chance
to come to New Jersey, of all states, and to northern
New Jersey at that, a scant ten or twenty miles
from Paterson and Rutherford and the Passaic
River, and do so with the right to select my own
"subject matter," I fear I was all too prepared to
make a choice. If what follows fails to do justice
to the achievement of Dr. William Carlos Williams —
for so long a man I have admired, read, and re-read —
then I think I know why. As President John F.
Kennedy once remarked, "life is unfair," and
neither talent nor wisdom by any means equally
bestowed upon us. If these lectures, if this book,
at least helps call attention to the stories and novels
looked at, I shall be grateful and feel the effort well
justified.

I wish to thank Mr. James Laughlin and his wife
for their friendship and hospitality. I would not have
felt able to take on this venture without their encouragement. For many years, of course, Mr. Laughlin
was Dr. Williams' friend as well as publisher; *Life*

Along the Passaic River, White Mule, and *In the Money* were issued by him: New Directions books. The entire Stecher trilogy is still in print as paperbacks because Mr. Laughlin knows what is valuable and important, and will stand by his judgment. I also wish to thank Mrs. William Carlos Williams for her kindness, good advice, and reassurance. It was a pleasure spending time with her in Rutherford. I am in debt to Professor Richard Schlatter of Rutgers for his repeated courtesies; and to Richard Poirier, of that university's English Department, I can only express the gratitude that a long-time friend feels for the privilege of knowing a person he very much respects and likes. Finally, I make mention of my wife and children; the dedication to them is not perfunctory, and not only an acknowledgement of "help" or "assistance" or "support." My wife for a long time has told our children about Dr. Williams, about what he wrote and stood for and struggled to accomplish. The boys have listened attentively, and so have I. In a sense, then, this book comes out of a family's spoken life.

Part One

The Passaic Stories

The Passaic Stories

America obsessed and haunted William Carlos Williams; he could not stop regarding its contradictions and ambiguities, its quite apparent wealth and power, its episodic idealism, its strong appetites — and its mean, self-centered, exploitative side. He never felt satisfied that he had, once and for all, grasped his native country, figured it out and come up with the words that would help others do so. No wonder *Paterson* defies categorization, for all the careful and subtle efforts made by the best-intentioned of friends and scholars.[1] Everyone agrees that the poem is a long and ambitious one; but as one tries to estimate exactly where Williams stands and what, finally, he upholds (in the way of doctrine, dogma, faith, or moral beliefs), the imposing turmoil of the poem and the extraordinary stretch of its author's imagination stand in the way. Both the narrator and his "subject matter" — people, places, things, and, not least, the social history of the United States — defy those whom, perhaps, Dr.

3

Williams had in mind as he wrote: the "intellectual heads," he once called them, who take evidence of inconsistency and confusion as a challenge, requiring yet another theoretical confrontation. The man who is Paterson brims with excitement, vitality, hopefulness. The man who is Paterson also shows himself to be tired, sad, forlorn, and soon enough ready for his last breath. The city which is Paterson grows, surges, carves out a destiny for itself. The city which is Paterson seems hopelessly doomed almost from the start. Now you see it, now you don't, the poet seems to be saying to his readers; just try and get a "viewpoint" or a "position" out of me (or out of the people I try to evoke, or out of the various situations I address myself to) and you will soon enough be brought up short or left unwittingly high and dry, with a forefinger pointing frantically at but one segment of territory; and such is the fate of those who are or want to be all too sure of themselves.

The child who became William Carlos Williams, poet, novelist, playwright, painter, essayist, inveterate letter-writer, librettist, social historian, and, not incidentally, a practicing physician for over a half a century, was born to parents whose "background" was unusual, and no doubt a source of occasional consternation for a growing boy. The father was English, the mother of Spanish, French and Jewish ancestry. As if to balance such an inheri-

tance, their son was born and died in Rutherford,
New Jersey—these days in America a remarkable
fact. But Dr. Williams in certain respects was
simply another American; there are elements of
fate and social circumstance in his family's past
which millions of Americans share, even if they are
never destined to live almost eight decades in one
state, never mind one town: a grandmother or-
phaned as a child and desperately poor, who nevertheless made her way across the Atlantic, and then
up the social ladder, and other relatives scattered in
various places outside or inside this country.
Williams was not alone when he contemplated the
mystery and magic of his existence—that a father
and mother of such different origins should even
have met.[2]

If a case can be made for the psychological basis
of Williams' never-ending interest in the social and
cultural forces that decisively shape human character, there is no reason to make a "case" of his
own life. Almost ravenously curious, never one to
sit back and stop taking the measure of others (or
himself), he nevertheless abstained from gestures
or long-term commitments which, to a degree,
would no doubt have appeased his quick and restless mind, so eager to travel so many roads. As a
boy he was taken to Europe, even sent to school in
Switzerland and France; and as a young man, and
later the father of two sons, he was not averse to a

return. But unlike Eliot and Pound, he mostly stayed home; more than that, he committed himself resolutely and unstintingly to the life of a small-town doctor. The demands upon him by his patients were constant, heavy, and hard, ethically, to rebuff —even when outrageous. He could never take a modest night's sleep for granted; and like all general practitioners (hence their declining number), he had to contend with those explosively irrational moments which patients have in the course of their day-to-day lives. Yet this man who loved New York City, and, especially in the 1920s, who was drawn to the literary and artistic life of Greenwich Village, never forsook Rutherford—thereby, one can say, facing up to the almost exquisite tensions of his life: all-night vigils beside struggling men, women and children, followed by a day of office hours and hospital rounds, and in between, a minute here, a minute there, notes to himself for poems, or the actual writing of them.

In *Paterson,* the reader is given precious few moments of abstraction—philosophical, theological, or literary. The contrast with Eliot's *Four Quartets* or Pound's *Cantos* is obvious, dramatic, and quite intentional. It is not simply a matter of case histories given, as in the fourth book: "M.N., a white woman aged thirty-five, a nurse in the pediatric ward, had no history of previous intestinal disturbance," and on and on. The section of Book

Two, titled "Sunday in the Park," which might have been an occasion for broad social comment, turns out to be as concrete and vivid as the particular lives of patients must have been for a doctor who was, really, a general practitioner, willing to go, day or night, on house visits, one of a dying breed. "Voices!" the poet exclaims, with reference to the people in the park. But he does not try to submit those voices to psychological or sociological generalization; they are "multiple and inarticulate," and in case we are unsettled or made impatient or inquisitive, Williams confronts us with a pause, a stretch of empty space, as if to say: stop and don't breathe heavy in expectation of an author's cool, sly analytic resolution of all this life he is trying to evoke. Then comes a period; and then a resumption, with "voices clattering loudly to the sun, to the clouds. Voices!/assaulting the air gaily from all sides."

The doctor who admitted time and again how cheated he felt by his patients — irreplaceable time lost — was the doctor who depended upon them for more than grist for his story-telling mill. Like Simone Weil, he could (*Paterson* II) refer to "the great beast"; but it is put in quotation marks: Alexander Hamilton's contemptuous reference to the ordinary men and women who, in his time by the thousands, and now by the millions, make up America. For Williams it is an occasion for irony; he

knows that the history of the city Paterson's seam-
ier, industrial side goes way back — in fact, to Hamilton, who, in 1791, as Secretary of the Treasury
under George Washington, helped found the Society
for Establishing Useful Manufactures, which was
located near present-day Paterson. From then on
New Jersey would be increasingly tied to the materialist, commercial ethic, though, of course,
Hamilton had no trouble dissociating himself from
such a development: let the lives of others make up
the "beast," and let a happy and privileged few do
the naming, the calling, the judging, thereby keeping themselves at a safe remove from the bestial.

Much has been made of Williams' tirades against
the academy and its various strictures or structures,
but I do not think, Williams himself at times not-
withstanding, that the issue was only T. S. Eliot's
Anglophilia, or his refusal to be bound by the localism which the author of *Paterson* or *Life Along the
Passaic River* or the Stecher trilogy so consistently
and ardently embraced. Nor is the issue a clear-cut
one of class and caste: the "aristocratic" interests of
Eliot and his followers, whose references, images,
and reflections direct one toward metaphysical
ideas, or the psychological anxieties of the well-to-
do which accompany the struggle to find "meaning"
in life, as against Williams' plain, ordinary working
people, who populate his Paterson and his fiction.
Williams was not so loyal to America that he didn't

ache for Europe. In a touching chapter of his autobiography he recalls how important it was on one
occasion for him and his wife to leave New Jersey —
to the point that they left their two young sons in
this country for over half a year with relatives. Nor
is Williams the proletarian poet and novelist who
turns factory workers or yeomen farmers into larger-
than-life heroes. Eliot's vision of the West's decline,
his sense that many of us are virtually dead, spiri-
tually, is not all that different from the portrait
Williams sometimes offers in *Paterson*. At one point
he refers to " a thousand automatons. Who because
they/neither know their sources nor the sills of
their/disappointments walk outside their bodies
aimlessly for the most part,/locked and forgot in
their desires — unroused."

Unlike Eliot, Williams feels a bond with his
automatons, has by no means given up on them.
Nor has he himself given up; *Paterson* was no preparation for an important religious conversion. But
what really distinguishes Williams from Eliot —
and from Ezra Pound — is his unrelenting insistence
on balance: he portrays sadness, desolation, evidence of decay everywhere, but he also gives us
decent, kind, and honorable people, who are energetic, thoughtful, and impressive enough as human
beings to warrant a good deal of attention from a
man of letters who cares to witness and write down
what there is to see and hear.

Williams was too shrewd an observer to deny the validity of the *Four Quartets* as a major philosophical and historical judgment by an extraordinarily gifted poet. The point, he knew, was to look elsewhere, look right around him. The "brown fog" Eliot refers to cannot be ignored. As those who travel on the Garden State Parkway know, Paterson often has plenty of fog, its eerie sulphurous quality perhaps worthy of the imagination of Eliot's hero, Dante. Yet there is more than bad air, violence, sexual hypocrisy, social discrimination, and economic injustice in northern New Jersey. Williams knew he could document the decline of the industrial West in one, as opposed to five, books. He believed, however, that in the midst of deceit, abandonment, exploitation, there is at least the possibility of love.

In Book Two of *Paterson*, the poet relentlessly exposes the way an economic system gone berserk becomes for various individuals a life of degradation. No one is spared—vulnerable and vulgar working people and their rich, corrupt bosses, whose particular cheapness, however gaudy and expensive, does not go unnoticed. Still, even though "among the working class SOME sort/of breakdown/has occurred"; even though "semi-roused/they lie upon their blanket/face to face," the poet feels inclined to turn on his own train of thought, maybe his own inclination as a social

critic, and continue this way: "mottled by the shad-
ows of the leaves/upon them, unannoyed,/at least
here unchallenged/Not undignified." He next asks
us to pause, with two periods — and one does indeed
wonder what more can be said about people, once
their dignity is acknowledged, even if a bit grudg-
ingly through a double negative. Williams was
never a miser; he simply knew how hard it is for
any of us to claim "dignity," in view of what we
are all asked to do again and again: compete, move
on up, get ahead — and on Sunday between eleven
and twelve pray for others left behind. He allows
himself to become neither rhetorical nor pietistic;
the dignity he has in mind is not the kind readily
mentioned by politicians and ministers. He keeps
his eyes wide open, declines an opportunity for
sentiment, but tries to indicate how, finally, at least
for moments, a number of us, in Patersons all over
the land, find a moment of affirmation: "talking,
flagrant beyond all talk/in perfect domesticity —/
and having bathed/and having eaten (a few/sand-
wiches)/their pitiful thoughts do meet/in the flesh —
surrounded/by churring loves! Gay wings/to bear
them (in sleep)/ — their thoughts alight,/away/ . . .
among the grass."

The complexity of such a psychological and sociological appraisal of ordinary Americans is hard for
many of us, raised on one or another ideology, to
accept without confusion and maybe, anger. And

our anger can prompt us to attribute confusion to
the poet: enough of his delicate tightrope walking;
let's examine "the system," and take for granted
(rather than point out as if a revelation) the unsym-
metrical and even contrary nature of just about
everyone's temperament. In Book Four, of course,
Williams does just that; he takes on Paterson's
bankers, factory owners, and managers in a way that
could only please his old friend Pound: "Money
sequestered enriches avarice, makes/poverty: the
direct cause of/disaster." Usury is his target:
" . . . Let credit/out. Out from between the bars/be-
fore the bank windows." But unlike Pound he will
not dwell on any single vice; and just as important,
he is wary of specific political and economic solu-
tions. He does permit himself this: ". . . Will you
consider/a remedy of a lot: i.e. LOCAL control of
local purchasing power./??/" Today, as suspicion
toward Washington, D.C., mounts, and as measures
like revenue-sharing attract support even from
liberals, such a suggestion must seem less fatuous
than it might have when first published, in June of
1951, when Harry Truman was doing his best to
keep the remnants of the New Deal intact. Williams
must have known why the owners of Texas oil wells
or Alabama cotton plantations or North Carolina
textile mills are anxious for the supremacy of a kind
of "local control." One has to assume that, funda-
mentally, he was asserting an anarchist position, for

all its shortcomings: opposition to the inequities
and dangers that are associated with the capitalist nation-state, that also go with Russia's state-
capitalism, and that, arguably, are associated with
all large-scale social and political "structures."

He was modest, maybe shrewdly restrained,
when he allowed himself economic analysis. Immediately after he has gone on a few pages about
credit and usury, in section two of Book Four, he
begins a new section with "Haven't you forgot your
virgin purpose,/the language?" The question was
obviously addressed to himself; his is primarily a
search for new ways of regarding the American
landscape and experience. But one wonders
whether Ezra Pound was not also being reminded
of something: he and Dr. Williams and others like
them have always known best how to strip us of
deceitful words, phrases, images, thereby hopefully providing a measure of truth—the clarity of a
poet's vision. If the children of Paterson, New
Jersey, sing "America the Beautiful," when their
stomachs are empty or their eyes tearing from sulphurous air or their bone marrow failing because of
lead poisoning contracted in a rat-infested tenement building, then someone's "virgin purpose"
ought to be a consideration of "the language"—the
flotsam and jetsam that is not confined to the Paterson or Passaic rivers but spills into classrooms and
churches and these days, every five minutes or so,

television screens: "better living through chem-
istry," "executive privilege," or something called
"the free world" (which includes Spain, South
Africa, South Korea, Brazil). The issue is words,
phrases and our response to them, our faith in them,
as well as such "structural" matters as the control
of "credit." Williams' much-discussed "localism"
was not only a matter of geography; he was no intellectual pygmy or political coward when he abstained
from preoccupations which would take him far
afield—metaphysical speculation, prescriptive (and
moralistic) political sociology. He would stay on his
particular territory and fight hard from there.

But he was capable of the bluntest social analysis. *Paterson* portrays, in Robert Lowell's words,
a country "grown pathetic and tragic, brutalized by
inequality, disorganized by industrial chaos, and
faced with annihilation." Northern New Jersey does
not lend itself to nature poetry; and one suspects
that even if Dr. Williams lived in Kansas or the
Pacific Northwest, he would not write poems like
William Stafford's. What George Orwell, by accident almost, happened to see as a patient in a Paris
hospital, and record unforgettably in "How the Poor
Die," Dr. Williams lived out every day as a protagonist: the doctor whose patients often enough had
no money, and little, if any, prospect of "success."
If there is beauty in such lives, it is not readily ap-

parent; moreover, as Williams kept insisting, it is not the kind our conventional language celebrates. Wider turnpikes, bigger airports, taller skyscrapers; they go to make up the urban or suburban "beauty" we are taught to appreciate: "renewal" — when in fact thousands of individuals and the homes they have tried to keep intact, against great odds, have been pushed aside by bulldozers. Our cameras, our wordy spokesmen or propagandists, don't seek and celebrate an old man's pride, an old woman's faith, a housewife's ingenuity and intelligence, her husband's almost desperate carpentry as it contends with "urban blight," a child's games or songs, whatever the ghetto or working-class neighborhood he calls home. Williams could not make up for the indifference of others, but he could approach "the roar, the roar of the present," and try to indicate who was making what noise, trying to get across which messages. Williams makes clear in his autobiography the tension he kept feeling between the commentator and the participant, between the physician who attends people, hence is all caught up in the rhythms of their life, and the poet who stands back and tries to condense, make things more pointed and suggestive. In *Paterson* the poet Noah Paterson may have, for once, enabled his creator to free himself of that tension; Noah is free to walk, hear and overhear, wax lyrical occasionally,

sigh more often, but then go ahead and practice
a kind of medicine, the pathologist's: an autopsy of
twentieth-century, industrial America.

Williams could only be introspective or abstract
in response to a concrete human situation or pre-
dicament. He was, again, the opposite of a metaphysical poet; he wondered about, worried over,
sang of, and no doubt dreamt of, the quite tangible
things of this world, as it is put, among which human beings qualify. His father was a staunch Uni-
tarian, and he himself never really strayed from the
kind of attentiveness to the here and now that
Emerson and Thoreau possessed. If there was to be
transcendence, and one keeps hoping and working
for it, then it will take place here on earth, in the
human mind: a new ordering of reality, a different
vision of what is possible.

Not until he was old and on the decline did he
give up his practice; in the last years of his life,
bedeviled by strokes, he himself became a patient.
When he was, finally, free of the burden other ail-
ing people placed on him, he still could not put
aside his efforts to locate them, himself, all of us:
man and woman in Paterson, in America, in this
particular century. "In old age/," he pointed out at
the beginning of *Paterson 5*, "the mind/casts off/
rebelliously/an eagle/from its crag. . . ." At first one
gets the impression this particular eagle would be
different from the four which preceded it — more

preoccupied with the problems of art and the artist: the creative struggle of generations of men and women who, like Henri de Toulouse-Lautrec (the poem is dedicated to him), had tried to witness faithfully the world and evoke it in a way that bestirs a viewer or reader to the point that he or she begins to see things differently. But midway in the poem — and significantly, in prose — we are told this: "It is no mortal sin to be poor — anything but this featureless tribe that has the money now — staring into the atom, completely blind — without grace or pity, as if they were so many shellfish." Mid-century America is living all too comfortably with the fake and the superficial; we have "come in our time to the age of the shoddy." More specifically: " . . . the men are shoddy, driven by their bosses, inside and outside the job to be done, at a profit." In contrast, there is " . . . the Portuguese mason, his own boss 'in the new country' who is building a wall for me, moved by old world knowledge of what is 'virtuous.' " Then the mason is given his voice: " . . . that stuff they sell you in the stores now-a-days, no good, break in your hands. That manufactured stuff, from the factory, break in your hands, no care what they turn out."

They had once again commanded his attention, the poor, humble people of northern New Jersey, and by extension America's working-class men and women. Despite the length and ambitiousness of

Paterson, there had been no extensive way for the poet William Carlos Williams to come to terms with the people seen day after day by the physician W. C. Williams. It is one thing to scan a city or region, highlight tersely its characteristics, and less sociologically, weave the language of ordinary people into the extraordinary statement, *Paterson.* But if one wants to approach those people more closely, in hopes of portraying the subtleties and intricacies of their lives, the development of their assumptions, the formation of their moral character, the pattern of their actions, then fiction becomes a strong temptation. It is not just a question of narration; some poems are indeed epic. A novel permits the writer wider latitude with individuals; they can go on and on — in their speech, in the decisions they make, the exertions they lend themselves to, the causes they may choose to pursue or oppose. Even a short story, for all its limitations, allows a more leisurely and detailed evocation of a particular segment of "life" — the examination of a given dramatic situation from a number of vantage points. The "Polock with his mouth open" or "the children with their dusty little minds and happiest *non sequiturs*" of *Paterson* 2 can become carefully drawn individuals as opposed to occasions for intensely highlighted images.

Williams worked on his fiction intermittently, but with great care. It took him years to complete the stories that go to make up *Life Along the Passaic River* (1938), most of which are directly drawn from his medical practice; and he wrote the sadly neglected but terribly important trilogy of *White Mule, In the Money,* and *The Build-Up* over a span of three decades. Those stories and novels are not the inadequate but pretentious offspring of a poet who didn't always know where his genius lay, even as some writers of strong fiction persist in throwing off every once in a while a poem or two, ensured publication by their reputation. The trilogy, in particular, haunted him; it is, in many respects, a fictional counterpart to *Paterson* — long, wide-ranging, closely connected to this nation's history, especially the social forces unleased by the industrialism of our Northeast. It can be said that fiction was for this particular writer a means of reconciliation — it was not in vain, the time spent in hospitals, in his office, on the road, going up the stairs of tenement houses to visit (so often) near penniless immigrants who were in pain, but who, often as not, distrusted fiercely the doctor they also knew they required. Rather, lives healed could become lives presented to others — and always, with Williams, made an occasion for moral instruction or ethical inquiry. The man who in 1925 published *In the American Grain,* with its brilliant evocations and interpretations of Cotton Mather, Abraham Lincoln, and the beginning of slavery in this coun-

try, was not one for "distance" from either his
"subjects" or the implications their lives might
have for those of us right now living ours.

Williams wrote about the working people who
live near the Passaic River at a time when sociological studies had yet to gain the dominance they
now have — as the almost matter-of-fact way that
readers choose for access to the lives of others.
George Linhart published *Out of the Melting Pot*,
a mixture of autobiography and fiction, in 1923, long
before the appearance of *Beyond the Melting Pot*,
the effort of Daniel P. Moynihan and Nathan Glazer
to examine sociologically the immigrant experience of the Irish, the Italians, the Jews, as well as
that of blacks and Puerto Ricans who have moved to
our cities more recently. Before Linhart there were
John Cournos' *Babel* (1922), Abraham Cohan's clas-
sic, *The Rise of David Levinsky* (1912), Theodore
Dreiser's *Jennie Gerhardt* (1911), Jack London's
powerful *People of the Abyss* (1903), Isaac Fried-
man's *Poor People* (1900), and back into the nineteenth century, Stephen Crane's *The Open Boat
and Other Tales of Adventure* (1899) and James
Sullivan's *Tenement Tales of New York* (1895).
There were the novels and stories of Edna Ferber
and Fannie Hurst; there were, also, Upton Sinclair's attempts to show how immigrants, as well
as native Americans, became hopelessly indentured
to the needs of an expanding economy: *King Coal*

and *Oil!* as well as his two-volume *Boston.* In 1917
a writer for *The New Republic* called such writing
"sociological fiction"—unaware, of course, that
quite soon, certainly from the time the Lynds' study
Middletown appeared onward, such fiction would
begin to diminish in impact—giving way, some
would say, to the various fictions of sociology and
other social sciences; the notion that with a ques-
tionnaire, or a spell of "field work," followed by the
extended resort to theoretical formulations, the
various and complicated thoughts and experiences
of many different kinds of people can be quite
adequately presented.[3]

In response, perhaps, novelists and even essayists began to pull back from "objective reality" and
concentrate their energies on exaggeration, distor-
tion, and escape: the weird, private fantasies of
their chosen characters, bizarre plots and subplots,
or the examination of the esoteric, the peculiar, or
the so-called mythic. What was the point of writing
about the poor, or the recently immigrated, when
growing numbers of "experts," claiming a range of
"techniques," and calling upon the almost un-
questioned authority of the social sciences, were
appearing here, there, and everywhere, and coming
up with something called "findings"? In contrast,
each of the nineteen stories in the collection *Life
Along the Passaic River* begins and ends without
the slightest promise of handy generalizations: "I

kept watching the Greek but he didn't look up, his face was like a board the whole time"; or, "Tried to get off her father's lap and fly at me while tears of defeat blinded her eyes." If there has to be a broader statement, Williams will occasionally oblige right off, as in this opening sentence: "He was one of those fresh Jewish types you want to kill at sight, the presuming poor whose looks change the minute cash is mentioned." In case the reader wants further elaboration about the "type" just characterized: "But they're insistent, trying to force attention, taking advantage of good nature at the first crack. You come when I call you, that type." As for the requirement that the social observer maintain both detachment and neutrality, here is a story teller's frank acknowledgement: "People like that belong in clinics, I thought to myself. I wasn't putting myself out for them, not that day anyhow. Just dumb oxen. Why the hell do they let them into the country. Half idiots at best. Look at them."

The story is "A Face of Stone," and with such a beginning one is hardly put in hopes of one of those "humanistic perspectives" today's college catalogues promise. A little more tolerance, or at least discretion, can even be found in the autobiographies of Michael Pupin, Edward Bok, and Andrew Carnegie, all three so full of themselves as self-declared successes, the poor immigrants who made good and therefore have a right to give lectures to

everyone else.[4] Williams is relentless in his description of the father and mother, and makes no
effort to conceal his own responses to what he saw:
"He got me into a bad mood before he opened his
mouth just by the half smiling, half insolent look
in his eyes, a small stoutish individual in a greasy
black suit, a man in his middle twenties I should
imagine." His wife "looked Italian"; she had "a
goaty slant to her eyes, a face often seen among
Italian immigrants." She was clutching the baby to
her; and the author easily could have set forth a
scene worthy of Käthe Kollwitz: the beleaguered,
confused, but animated and proud mother holding
a child who comes across as innocent, vulnerable,
appealing. Instead we are told that the mother had
"no expression at all on her pointed face, unless
no expression is an expression. A face of stone. It
was an animal distrust, not shyness." In the event
anyone is still ready to romanticize or idealize the
woman, the author tells us that there was a great
deal of dirt under her nails, that "she smelled," and
that the smell is the kind "you find among many
people who habitually do not wash or bathe."

The child was a mere infant of five months, the
doctor notices. We are given no account of the baby
boy, though — only further grumbling and worse
from the doctor: "Well what do you want me to
do? To hell with you, I thought to myself. Get sore
and get the hell out of here. I got to go home to

lunch." Not exactly a Norman Rockwell scene; and by this time one is entitled to remember that the particular physician happens to be a poet—hence, presumably, a doubly sensitive and thoughtful person. He comes across as at the very least gruff; in 1974 we might want to call him a bigot, a racist, a pig, and on and on. Moreover, it turns out that there isn't anything wrong with the child. ("I couldn't find much the matter and told them so.") We are denied a plot wherein pain and suffering finally melt a somewhat crusty, narrow-minded, or harassed American physician, who slowly, as he struggles against serious illness, gains an understanding of and respect for these strange, alien parents. The doctor brusquely offers " a complemental formula"; the baby is the mother's first and she, like many others, is inexperienced at feeding— though the doctor in his private thoughts about her doesn't grant her that company, that "explanation" for her behavior, because if he did the tone of the story would be quite different. Immediately after the formula is offered we are told that the father "chiseled a dollar off the fee."

The story has just begun, of course, when the parents leave the doctor's office with their baby son. They have, in their own way, established themselves as patients; in case of trouble they want to feel able to return. The physician is still suspicious, however; in our contemporary way of putting things, he not too subtly "rejects" them, shows his "hostility" toward them, by emphasizing that he doesn't like to make house calls at supper time or in the midst of bad weather or "at two o'clock in the morning." Anyway, he is already much too busy. The couple leave, convinced in their minds that they have a doctor who will help them when needed. They seem oblivious to the implicit and explicit annoyance, at the very least, that doctor feels toward them. Nor are their contacts by phone going to work out any better: "And sure enough, on a Sunday night, about nine o'clock, with the thermometer at six below and the roads like a skating rink, they would call me." The answer, we are told, was "nothing doing." They would not, however, take that for an answer. Eventually the doctor hangs up, to the horror of his wife: "You musn't do that." We are almost mid-way in the story, and at an impasse: a blunt, uncivil doctor and a young, working-class immigrant family who can, according to the tastes of the reader, be considered petulant and ignorant, or earnestly unsophisticated but possessed of their own, stubborn, unyielding dignity.

Suddenly it is "four months later." The doctor admits to "three months of miserable practice." Finally a touch of spring has arrived: "the first warm day in April." He has some twenty sets of mother and child to see, so no pleasant spell outside for him. Just as he is finishing up they appear, the three

of them: "the same fresh mug and the same face of
stone, still holding the baby which had grown, however, to twice its former size." The doctor almost
fails to recognize them at first, then impatiently (or
rudely, it can be claimed) he asks them what
prompted the visit. ("Make it snappy cause I've got
to get out.") They have no particular complaint,
just the wish that their son receive a checkup. The
doctor is, predictably, angered. He motions to them
to put the child upon his examining table, all the
while noticing that the child, in fact, looks in excellent condition, whereas his father has "a cluster
of red pimples" on his face. As the mother, presumably, is undressing her baby, the doctor and
father talk — a conversation quite like thousands that
take place every day in the offices of pediatricians
all over America. How far to go along with the
infant's demands? What kind of food to introduce at
what age? Where should the child sleep — nearby,
or off by himself? Finally, the mother has undressed
her son and handed him over for inspection: "Getting up I went to the infant and pulled the shoes and
stockings off together, picked the thing up by its
feet and the back of the neck and carried it to the
scales." The mother hovers close by, too close. The
doctor is ready to tell her off. By now the story is
well over half done, and the tone seems relentlessly
consistent. But suddenly there is a slight turn in
direction: " . . . the child grinned and sagged back

unresisting in my grasp." He relaxes with the boy
and regards him afresh: "a smart looking little thing
and perfectly happy fresh mug on him that amused
me in spite of myself."

Things are not going to change all that dramatically, however. The story goes briskly on; the doctor does not reflect on the reason he has been, to a
degree, at least, brought up short. "Twenty pounds
and four ounces," he announces. Then he tersely
lets the parents know that there is nothing wrong
with their child. At the same time, he cannot resist
a rather suggestive (and insulting) question: "What
do you want for a ten months old baby?" Until
this point the father has been an intermediary, the
one who conveys his wife's hopes and fears to a
doctor both irascible and very much needed. He
has been a tactful man, a father just appealing
enough, it seems, to ward off a real explosion. Now
the mother speaks out—and with more directness
and insistence than the reader (and one will soon
learn, the doctor) has any reason to expect: "I want
you should examine him first." For the doctor there
was nothing to say, only this to let the rest of us
know: "the blood went to my face in anger." Then
he adds: "but she paid no attention to me." In fact,
she went right on and without any apologies: "He
toothin."

In a marvelously ironic twist, Williams has the
doctor acknowledge that he picked up his steth-

oscope and examined the child's chest "to quiet
my nerves." He finds nothing wrong, tells the
mother and father so, and tries to regain both his
composure, and by this time, the offensive in what
seems to be a story about the war of nerves that can
go on between a general practitioner from one kind
of background and patients who almost literally
speak another tongue. The parents are told to "step
on it." "Get him dressed," they hear. And finally,
the emphasis of personal confession: "I got to get
out of here." Nothing doing, the mother indicates
with her quick rejoinder of a question: "Him all
right?" The doctor now notices her "stony pale
green eyes" — and again there is a shift in his attitude and in the tone of narration. The eyes are
described as "very curious," as "almost at right
angles to each other," and not least, like those "of
female figures I had seen somewhere — Mantegna —
Botticelli — I couldn't remember."

The sophisticated intellectual, in this instance
long responsive to art, has found at least something
about (some part of) his patient interesting and
attractive. Among many of the working people who
live along the Passaic River "the eyes are the windows of the soul." I recall a factory worker who
lives in Haverhill, Massachusetts, near the Merri-
mack River, one very much like the Passaic — that is,
hopelessly polluted — telling me that he and his
wife always judged people by their eyes: "we look

at a person's eyes, and we decide if he's honest and good, or if he isn't. You have your shifty-eyed people, and your people who look right at you, because they don't have a thing to conceal. I've known some people, I don't like the looks of them; but we'll be talking, and suddenly I see by their eyes that they're alright, they're not crooks, and they mean well. I can't explain it any more."

Nor is Williams about to become introspective or wordy; he can't quite "remember," make a specific connection between this (at best, to him) pitiable mother and a Renaissance painting or piece of sculpture, but he has been prompted to regard her, at least partially and for a second, as if she lived elsewhere, spoke a different kind of English, dressed differently, and on and on. A second later, of course, he is all business, answering her question about her child and preparing to nudge her and her husband and child out of the office. Perhaps the story could have been brought to a conclusion at this point: a face of stone, but interesting eyes, and maybe a final, polite goodbye which indicates the beginning of a less tempestuous relationship between the doctor and the parents of his young patient. Instead, the mother herself becomes a patient; her husband suddenly asks that his wife be examined. There is yet another outburst; the doctor acknowledges that he "turned on him." Little was held back: "What the hell do you think I am anyhow. You got a hell of a nerve. Don't you know. . . ." But the husband again persists, and the result is a temporary stalemate. "I could hardly trust myself to speak for a moment," the doctor observes. He also cannot quite bring himself to walk out of his office. He is conscientious as well as thoroughly annoyed. And a continuing, below-the-surface curiosity works at him. His eyes, which had noticed her eyes, begin their work again: "I looked her coldly up and down from head to toe." He notices a rip in her dress. He notices her face and her body; she is, on the whole, an awkward appearing, rather unattractive woman. Soon he has quieted down enough to speak; he has become as philosophical as many of his patients in the course of their lives become: "no use getting excited with people such as these — or with anyone, for that matter. . . ." He returns to his desk chair. No doubt reaching for a pad of paper, he asks the inevitable doctor's question: "What's the matter with her?"

The lady experiences pain in her legs, worse at night. There is a spot of sorts on her right knee. The doctor refines his questions. Has she ever had rheumatism? Have her joints swollen up? The questions are addressed to the husband, and meant for his wife. The answers come back from him: "She don't know, he said. . . ." Then come instructions: open the dress, sit down, extend your legs. They turn out to be quite bowed, "really like Turkish scimitars." She has had rickets. She has a broken varicose vein. Moreover, she is wearing the worst possible shoes. There is no cure for bow legs, and nothing to be done just yet about the varicose vein, but a new pair of sensible shoes is quite within the range of possibility, even for a poor couple. As he makes his recommendation the doctor asks the man how old his wife is. She is twenty-four. The man is asked where his wife was born. She is from Poland—a great surprise to the doctor. He'd never placed her there: "an unusual type for a Jew," he thinks. He now tries to address her directly. Was she "a kid of maybe five or six years" during the war? She is unwilling to respond. Those eyes of hers now strike him differently as he comments that she "just looked back into my eyes with that inane look."

All along, as the doctor has been directing questions at the woman through her husband, the reader has been told, virtually each time, that the poor man, for all his determination that his wife get proper care, is himself not comfortable with the English language, and keeps on blushing. It is obvious that he does not blush out of anger or resentment. When the doctor gets tough with him, he simply holds on tenaciously to what he believes his rights are: to ask, and ask again for help; to explain yet another time what ails his child, and later, his wife. But when he speaks on his own initiative about his wife, or when he carries back to the doctor information she has offered, usually in response to a medical question, the reader is told that the man appears "red in the face." We are never going to get a precise explanation of why the man reacts so. We do get, however, a sudden, if limited change in the office atmosphere. There is a shift from medical to social inquiry. Her bow legs, the doctor realizes, were the result of war and famine. He wants to know what she remembers eating as a child. When she doesn't seem to hear, he asks whether she lost relatives, "any of her people," and through her husband obtains an answer: "she lost everybody." Well, not quite; as has so often been the case, for millions of immigrants, one member of the family had come over here before the awful disaster took place – a war, followed by an epidemic, followed by a pogrom. The doctor is ready to stop thinking about symptoms; he has finally caught a glimpse of a particular person. The mother is utterly absorbed with her child, he realizes; she has no eyes for him, even if he is possessed of awesome authority and knowledge. Having lost everyone and everything, the baby for her is the beginning of new life. Her appearance, in contrast, must be a constant reminder of an earlier life: "No wonder she's built the way she is, considering what she must have been through in that invaded territory."

He does not dwell on this new-found empathy.

For one thing, her ever alert, solicitous, and (if need be) outspoken husband is right there, ready with other questions: for instance, what will the doctor do about the woman's leg pain? The answers are given briskly, but without evident impatience or irritation. Good shoes will help. Eventually an operation for removal of the varicose veins could be done, but not now. Better to get some snug fitting bandages, which will help return the venous circulation to the heart. The couple for the first time is being treated with consideration; they are receiving neither pity nor condescension. Of course, the doctor's attitude is not going to become, right off, his patients'. He knows that given the right shoes and the use of the bandages he recommended, the pain felt by the young mother would recede or disappear outright. He knows also that he is asking them to be forebearing and to buy something which doesn't in their minds lend itself to immediate hope —as, say, a pill would. He has tried to reach out from his own condition, as existentialist philosophers would put it, to that of others; or more sociologically, he has tried to transcend the barriers of class. More work will be required, as the husband indicates quickly, but with noticeable restraint (a tacit acknowledgment of the new courtesy he has been receiving). A touch petulantly he asks, "Can't you give her some pills to stop the pain?"

No, the doctor won't go along with that; from his

vantage point there is the danger of addiction. As
he responds to the request, we learn how hard it is
for social attitudes to be put aside, even in the so-
called "scientific" atmosphere of a clinician's
office. "Not me, I told him," says the doctor immediately—as if his pride were at stake: you may
find other doctors who go along with such a request,
and thereby show themselves flawed or compro-
mised, but "not me." Then, as if he senses, rather
than exactly realizes, what he has been showing
about himself (and his view of "them," the different ones in various respects, who have sought
him out), he pulls back into a more flexible position: "You might get her teeth looked at, though, if
you want to. All that kind of thing and—well, I will
give you something. It's not dope. It just helps if
there's any rheumatism connected with it."

There is no response to that mixture of explanation, self-righteousness, and apology. Still unable
to shake off a set of assumptions, but now at least
and at last ready to turn to the woman directly,
rather than go through her husband, the doctor
asks, "Can you swallow a pill?" She is quite willing,
at this point, to speak for herself. She shifts ground
slightly by asking "how big?" She has shrewdly
refused to answer the question precisely—and by
implication, whether the reply is yes or no, she has
also refused to dignify an inquiry bound to reveal
her ignorant or at a lack, if she admitted she couldn't

take pills, or unnecessarily self-protective if she bellowed, as she had every right to, *what do you mean can I swallow a pill!* The husband feels the need, for the last time, it turns out, to intervene: "She swallows an aspirin pill when I give it to her sometimes," he begins. Then he adds: "but she usually puts it in a spoonful of water first to dissolve it." With that account, meant to help the doctor, the man blushes. We are told by the doctor that "suddenly I understood his half shameful love for the woman and at the same time the extent of her reliance on him." And in a separate line given the authority of a paragraph: "I was touched." Here again the story might have been ended, maybe with a line or two of "fade-out": the departing couple, the doctor newly aware and thoughtful; in sum, a barrier or two, out of millions that exist, broken down. But Williams seems interested in pursuing the matter, the situation, a bit further. The husband has become quite adept at dealing with his "betters"; if "they" want to know something, tell them—in enough detail to satisfy their particular kind of hunger; maybe, then, one's own hunger will get attention paid to it. The man's evident embarrassment, his redness of face, indicates that something has happened to undo his truculent reserve. The woman's "face of stone" has, after all, been one of three; the doctor has been rather grim (perhaps the image might be changed anatomically, and the description stony-hearted used) and the husband has had his own kind of "face of stone" — the inscrutability which the doctor-narrator has at last penetrated with his interpretation.

But the woman has no "shame"; moreover, her "reliance" on her husband turns out to be not so complete. Williams has to all appearances finished his story when he has the doctor take stock of the couple psychologically; in the original edition of *Life Along the Passaic River* (New Directions, 1938), the reader is on the top of the last page, and it is less than half filled with words. After tersely but pointedly confiding that he was touched, that he had only begun to know his patients for the first time, the doctor quickly moves back to the office scene: "They're pretty big pills," he announces, speaking of the medicine he is about to prescribe. Since he has become, after a fashion, won over, he demonstrates a hitherto missing solicitude. He explains that the pills are green, because they are coated with a substance that helps them get easily digested. Suddenly, a few lines from the end, the woman emerges: "Let see." The doctor obliges. She has more to say, to ask: "For pains in leg?" The doctor tells her yes. She scrutinizes the pills, and then reveals "a broad smile," the first one her observant physician had noticed. And next, the last words of the story — hers: "Yeah," she speaks out, "I swallow him."

It is, perhaps, tempting to make much out of "him": a moment in which a mistake, based on lack of ease with English, comes across (to this psychological-minded age) as a "slip" of sorts — the doctor and his medicine, as it were, merged in the patient's mind. I think it best to give the woman every benefit of the doubt. Maybe she did, without knowing it, indicate that at last she, like her doctor, was "touched"; she, like him, had finally "understood," and so felt prepared for an act of acceptance. If one gets all caught up in that vein of psychological analysis, there is a good chance that another kind of psychology will be overlooked. The doctor-narrator has, in fact, told us a story about an ignorant, superstitious woman whose husband at least was able to help her out when it came to dealing with doctors and lawyers if not Indian chiefs: the range of people who populate American life, and whose "services" even a self-absorbed, poor, and illiterate immigrant will call upon from time to time. She proved that she didn't always have "a face of stone," and she showed the doctor's estimate of her "personality" to be in error. His surmise that she relied so heavily upon her husband turns out to be less helpful than one had thought. In the last moments of this story she exhibits a side of herself until then not apparent. She is quick to assert herself, brisk and pointed in speech, and quite able to manage on her own. She is not the woman whose fears and inade-

quacies just moments earlier in that office prompted
at the very least exasperation in her doctor and
repeated evidence of shame in her necessarily
protective husband. She proves the characterization "A Face of Stone" inaccurate, and she ends
up having the last, quite definitive word — an ironic
twist.

I have given the story a rather close reading because doing so brings up a number of issues about
the "life" which Dr. Williams attended to as a
physician and attempted to sketch out in his stories.
"A Face of Stone" is like the others in *Life Along
the Passaic River;* the reader is confronted with a
blunt, at times abrasive if wise physician who
clearly knows his way around, but who seems, at
times, ready to throw in the towel: all those demands from all those people. They are working-
class people, men and women just over from one or
another European country, or born here of distinctly
humble origin. The full force of black and Puerto
Rican migrations had not touched New Jersey in the
1920s and 1930s; some blacks do figure in *Paterson*
and *Life Along the Passaic River,* though not at
all in the trilogy that portrays the fate of the Stecher
family — *White Mule, In the Money,* and *The Build-
Up.* The narrator of the Passaic stories is a physician
who obviously gets to come in contact with those
struggling men and women (whom many of us today, not felicitously, refer to as "ethnics") in a

rather special way. I suppose it can be said that,
whether he knew it or not, Williams was a social observer who had an extraordinarily special "relationship" with his "subjects," and who thereby became
privy to their aspirations, hesitations, and worries
as no other outsider did.

We know what he did with that "relationship";
for one thing, he took it for granted, while all the
while rendering an important service: the doctor's
job. He also, quite clearly, had his own, personal
ax to grind, as one after the other, the patients came
into his office, or appeared before him on hospital
beds as he made his rounds. He very much wanted
and needed to be a physician, enjoyed being able to
summon that mixture of authoritative competence
and solicitude which earns respect from men,
women, and children otherwise, for many reasons,
inclined to suspicion, if not outright resentment.
Often the doctor who narrates the Passaic stories
stops suddenly and becomes "philosophical"; in
"A Face of Stone" he found himself observing that
there was "no use getting excited with people such
as these — or with anyone, for that matter." He describes himself as thinking such a thought "in
despair," but the characterization seems both inaccurate and misleading. He has in fact begun to
feel better about the individuals who just seconds
earlier had vexed him so; and he has profited per-
sonally from his dealings with them, as doctors,

including psychiatrists, sometimes do. Only someone who knows that at times he gets "excited" by
people for reasons that have little to do with their
actions, and rather much to do with his own temperament, is likely to add the significant qualification "or with anyone." "At times," remarked Harry
Stack Sullivan, "I am listening especially hard to
my own words or thoughts, because it is I who
ought pay attention as well as the individuals I am
speaking with."

But if Williams was a healer, an observer, a man
working out "there" in some sociological or anthro-
pological "field," he was, all the time (by his own
description) a writer, and it is particularly important to compare his "approach," and even more
ponderously, his "methodological procedures"
with those of the social scientists who have had
their own reasons to be interested in people like
those who live in the various "communities" which
adjoin New Jersey's Passaic river. To begin with,
the woman with "a face of stone" sought out the
doctor, rather than vice versa; she had a young
child who, to her mind, was in trouble. The doctor
was not just any doctor, but a respected baby doctor,
well spoken of. And regardless of the doctor's
office manners, or in other stories, his bedside
manner, it doesn't take him long to get down to
business. He may be less forthcoming than some of
his patients would like, less given to long and

patient explanations, less reassuring, and certainly not soothing, at least in a direct way; but he is quick to give commands which indicate a thorough willingness to work, and work hard against whatever disease or "problem" is brought to him. "Well, put it up there on the table and take its clothes off then," he tells the couple in "A Face of Stone." If he doesn't offer the kind of consolation one *thinks* his patients want, he at least proves himself conscientious and available, even if he does tell the couple in the story we have looked at not to bother him impulsively at all hours of the day or night. But they, anyway, are not put off; and as the doctor tells of his wife's surprise at his firmness if not toughness on the phone, one gathers that he does not customarily go even that far. Moreover, we have in the beginning of the story learned that the doctor has had good cause to appraise the couple and realize that they are more than a match for any thickness of skin he happens to demonstrate to them. Faces of stone are not fragile flowers; and the husband, in the story's second sentence, is described as "insistent," and as "trying to force attention." In fact, he is "you come when I call you, that type."

In several stories, "Jean Beicke," for instance, the protagonist is an infant child whose parents or other relatives scarcely appear — and still the doctor gets irritable or moody, and says things to himself (and his readers) which no self-respecting social scien-

tist doing "field work" and writing up his "findings" would dare say, at least so directly. Jean
Beicke is only eleven months old, and surely if he
could find nothing positive to say, her doctor might
have refrained from being critical about her appearance. But he begins the story by talking about
the Great Depression and the "unwanted children"
it has spawned: workers out of jobs, mothers unable
to count on money for food and clothing, never
mind toys or games. He won't, it seems, become
tender and sympathetic as he talks about those parents and their children; nor will he become the
indignant political moralist: America the badly
run nation, whose economic system, run amok, is
driving millions of vulnerable human beings to
distraction and worse. "The parents," he comments
at the beginning of "Jean Beicke," "sometimes
don't even come to visit them, afraid we'll grab
them and make them take the kids out, I suppose."
As for those "kids," they often strike their doctor as
"stinking dirty, and I mean stinking." He also talks
of "poor brats" — and, in reference to the infant
Jean, "one of the damndest looking kids I've ever
seen." Her head was flattened, we are told, and her
legs and arms hung loose, like those "of some cheap
dolls."

Such descriptions are scarcely objective; they
might even be called "prejudiced" rather than
merely subjective. If anything, Dr. Williams is

restrained in "A Face of Stone." In "Jean Beicke" he seems to have in mind deliberate provocation of his readers' liberal, middle-class sensibility. When he praises the nurses, he does so at the expense, one could argue, of the children they try to help: "You ought to see those nurses work. You'd think it was the brat of their best friend." The word "brat" is a warning signal; just a few sentences on there is a surprising acknowledgment: the nurses "break their hearts over those kids, many times, when I, for one, wish they'd never get well." He continues, a bit later, with more tough talk, this time rather rude and vulgar in tone: "I looked at some miserable specimens they've dolled up for me when I make the rounds in the morning and I tell them: Give it an enema, maybe it will get well and grow up into a cheap prostitute or something. The country needs you, brat. I once proposed that we have a mock wedding between a born garbage hustler we'd saved and a little female with a fresh mug on her that would make anyone smile."

Why such casual, almost brutish remarks from a poet of such tenderness and thoughtfulness, the poet of "Blue Flags" ("I stopped the car/to let the children down/where the streets end/in the sun/") or of "The Lonely Street" ("School is over. It is too hot/to walk at ease. At ease/in light frocks they walk the streets/to while the time away./")? Poor Jean Beicke; she is quite ill, and soon enough she

dies. The story is, really, an account of a doctor's
losing struggle. It is also a frankly confessional
account: "We did everything we knew how to do
except the right thing." At no point, for all his
apparent arrogance toward the mostly unemployed
working class people, does the doctor become self-
righteous, or even, as doctors are not incapable of
being, self-protective. There was no question of
deliberate or casual wrong-doing; the child was
treated quite conscientiously and intelligently,
one gathers. But in the face of a worsening infec-
tion, which began to affect the central nervous
system, the doctor failed, in the little time available, to pin down the source of the fulminating illness. He becomes a touch impersonal when he
mentions that "nobody thought to take an x-ray of
the mastoid regions," where an autopsy eventually
revealed an acute infectious process; but he is not
about to fob off blame on others: "We might, however, have taken a culture of the pus when the ear
was first opened," he remarks, and then, moving
ever closer to himself (from "nobody" to "we" to
"I") he promises that "I shall always, after this, in
suspicious cases" do just that.

He had actually become quite fond of the infant
girl. In the same paragraph which tells us that he
"had to laugh" when he looked at his tiny patient,
because she was so "funny looking," we also learn
that "we all got to be crazy about Jean." But Wil-

liams is exquisitely contrapuntal as he conveys the tangle of his responses to the child. However "crazy" he was about her, he will not allow the story to slip into sentiment; it is as if he knows that his readers want just that development to take place — the unfortunate one who never had a chance, and who finally won over her crusty doctor, so full of cynicism and weariness, before she died. As in the case of the woman with "a face of stone," there is a gradual recognition of the child's dignity, accompanied, however, by the decided persistence of the original perceptions the reader has been given — almost as if the writer wants to make it quite clear that the misery and wretchedness he sees, and tries to envisage for his readers through the use of words, will not yield to intimate acquaintance or compassionate involvement.

As Jean Beicke lay dying, her doctor acknowledges that, "Somehow or other, I hated to see that kid go." Not only him, but others; in fact, "everybody felt rotten." Immediately, however, he says again, as strongly as ever, what he thought of the child: "She was such a scrawny, misshapen, worthless piece of humanity that I had said many times that somebody ought to chuck her in the garbage chute. . . ." True, he no longer felt quite like that. But he doesn't apologize for his past feelings, nor does he "compensate" for them, as psychologists or psychiatrists would put it, by stressing unduly

the new view of Jean which he has come upon.
Mixing clinical observation with just a touch of
emotion, he says that "after a month watching her
suck up her milk and thrive on it—and to see those
alert blue eyes in that face—well, it wasn't pleasant." Those last few words, of course, amount to a
considered understatement. At this point the story
might have been brought to a close—as it was also
possible for the author to do in "A Face of Stone":
the doctor at last in touch emotionally with his
patient, and on that account possessed of a larger
degree of self-awareness. But Williams won't have
it so. He moves us back to a more detached position by reminding us of the sad if not sordid circumstances which characterize "life along the
Passaic River": the mute and half-destroyed mother
of Jean; the aunt who tells the doctor that the
child's father has taken off with another woman;
the severe straits the mother was in, jobless in the
midst of a terrible economic depression and without any real support from anyone, including her
runaway husband, now in Canada. On the other
hand, he lets emerge out of that sadness and hopelessness a contradictory theme: the tact, intelligence, generosity, and goodwill of people who in
their quiet, patient, obliging way make a contrast
with—him, actually. Jean's mother cries "without
a sound" as she watches life ebb away from her
child. Jean's aunt speaks of her sister's grim situa-

tion in a subdued, clear-headed, disarming manner. Moreover, when the doctor with understandable hesitation, brings up the subject of permission for an autopsy, the aunt is forthright and sensible: "If you can learn anything, it's only right." Nor is the aunt going to have any trouble with her sister; the child's mother, the doctor is told, "won't make any kick."

Dr. Williams does not need to draw a detailed comparison with the attitude many far better off (and better speaking) individuals might have. But he does choose to end his story in a somewhat surprising, if not suggestive way; and so doing, he makes "poverty" as much a source of self-confrontation for the well-to-do as it is a "problem" for "them," the poor. At the autopsy his clinical hunch is confirmed; he had indeed made the mistake he suspected. He calls up a colleague of his, an otolaryngologist, to tell him of his mistake: "A clear miss." The ear doctor responds unmercifully to both of them: "If we'd gone in there earlier, we'd have saved her." At that, the doctor is moved to anger, not in extenuation of his own failure in judgment, but for the same reason, one suspects, he has been as curt, agitated, and cynical all along: "For what?" he asks. Save the child for the misery ahead of her, by virtue of who she is, where she lives, what her parents have, or better, don't have, to offer her? He doesn't ask that kind of explicit, long-

winded and preachy question. He follows his "For
what?" with a terse: "Vote the straight communist
ticket." And he has his nameless colleague, also
upset by his own clinical misjudgment, end the
story with a comment upon that rather unexpected
political recommendation: "Would it make us any
dumber?"

A certain kind of "field-worker" and social observer chooses to "write up" his experiences in
the form of stories which, repeatedly, must strike
some of us as needlessly harsh, and upon occasion,
gratuitously pessimistic. The "stone face" relaxes,
but clearly she is to be, forever, deformed; as for
her son, he is quite sick and by no means an appealing child, one day to be a Horatio Alger, now that
his parents are in New Jersey rather than a ghetto
in Poland. Jean Beicke will never live to see the
Passaic river become even more polluted, its
nearby towns even more crowded and, in time,
plagued by various social and racial tensions. On
the other hand, the Great Depression did end, so
no doubt a practicing physician who lived in Rutherford, New Jersey, today and worked among the
people who live nearby, and wrote stories based on
that work, would certainly not mention the Communist party — a metaphor for an utterly antagonistic
political position *vis-à-vis* America's capitalist
system, of which northern New Jersey is more than
a mere outpost. Yet, one suspects, he would crave

some metaphor, some gesture of disagreement, if not outrage: that the considerable social injustice the doctor-writer has in mind, the dumbness the otolaryngologist makes reference to, have by no means disappeared.

It is the genius of these stories that they are utterly concrete, yet lend themselves, without any help from the author in the form of discursive asides, to social comment or political analysis. Dr. Williams wants to carry his readers along, as any writer does, through one plot, then the next, thereby capturing their imaginations, and not incidentally, bringing them closer to a certain kind of "life." But he also seems to judge himself a reader—a relatively comfortable and well-educated person who lives quite another kind of "life" than that portrayed in these stories of his. He struggles constantly to bring himself closer to people who, at the same time, he openly acknowledges disliking or not understanding. He misjudges us, we may insist; even as he did both the lady of "stone face" and the infant Jean. We are broader, more knowing, more tolerant, than he allows. Or is it more important to emphasize that apart from anyone's particular psychological makeup, the readers of these stories, like their author, are thoroughly "above" those industrial workers—or those castoffs our social and economic order has no apparent inhibition from generating? Put differently, the power is ours—the

capacity and willingness to type or classify others,
and mull over (and act upon) various "approaches"
to them: studies, analyses, research projects, pro-
grams, "strategies for intervention," and on and on.
Meanwhile those "others" are indeed inscrutable,
as the lady was. The doctor's power is naturally not
in and of itself malignant; but he does possess
more power than he really cares to (or dares to?)
acknowledge. To call upon theological language,
only gradually does his pride, the sin of sins, become evident — and never, fully, to himself. The
reader is presumably made uneasy in proportion to
the doctor's reluctant and incomplete self-scrutiny:
in his office he was too quick to judge the couple,
and he stumbled fatally (so far as Jean's life went)
in the pediatric ward.

For all the subtlety of Williams' stories, for all
his credentials as the authority, the good doctor and
adroit writer and shrewd essayist who weaves into
his stories a whole range of social comment, at no
point does he emerge as a thoroughly self-possessed
person — the researcher who has gone "out there,"
and yes, stumbled, badly sometimes, but eventually
come home with his pockets full of discoveries and
self-discoveries, summaries and conclusions and
recommendations — to "us," who will (he believes,
we believe) read his reports, papers, monographs
and ultimately, "important" books. Rather, he
remains unchanged, and not especially authorita-

tive: personal rather than didactic, and quite tenta-
tive about a world he can only regard with mixed
feelings — strong admiration for the endurance of
people who (he believes) are most likely, at the
most, barely going to survive the vicissitudes await-
ing them, but also a kind of angry regret: that
people should have to live so marginally, and that
he should have to spend so much time contending
with the frustrations a doctor like him must face
when his practice is made up of hard-pressed and
often near penniless families.

What is Williams trying to do in these stories?
They are not really confessional, for all the ac-
knowledgments he makes about himself and how
he reacted to others. They are not ambitiously
definitive: here are your factory workers, lock,
stock, and barrel. "America is hard to know," he has
one of his characters say, and since the story ("The
Venus") comes toward the end of the book, we are
especially grateful, because that is what the cu-
mulative effect of various events, incidents, encounters and situations seems to convey. In another
story ("Danse Pseudomacabre") the musing narrator asks: "How can a man live in the face of this
daily uncertainty? How can a man not go mad with
grief, with apprehension?" Perhaps at times he
answered those questions by reminding himself
that he was the poet, the one who *sees* — on behalf
of others as well as himself: "Sunshine fills the out-

of-doors, great basins of it dumped among factories standing beside open fields, into backlots, upon a rutted baseball field, into a sewage ditch running rain water, down a red dirt path to four goats." But the same story ("The Accident") aims to account for the survival of others. And so, as the doctor comforts his infant son, who has fallen, there are others nearby, who also look closely at the world, or at the very least, make do: "In the windows of the Franco-American Chemical Co. across the way six women have appeared in two windows, four in one and two in the other. They watch the baby, wondering if he is hurt. The linger to look out. They open the windows. Their faces are bathed with sunlight. They continue to strain out at the window. They laugh and wave their hands. Over against them in an open field a man and a boy on their hands and knees are planting out slender green slips in the fresh dirt, row after row. We enter the car. The baby waves his hand. Goodbye!"

A touch romantic—perhaps in the vein of the William Carlos Williams who, around 1913, painted a quite bucolic Passaic river? Yes, but part of the truth, that quite ambiguity-filled truth of the "life" Williams saw around him. One moment (in "The Right Thing") a child is "fairly eating me up with her cold, steady eyes and no expression to her face whatever." Another time we are asked to share a doctor's awe: "It has puzzled me for years to solve the dignity of this shabby figure, a steady worker, a silent walker in the worst storms, incredibly resistant, in wide-open shoes, solitary. . . ." The man works as a gardener and handyman. His father was a gardener, too. Does the psychologically sensitive reader want more "family history"? Well, there is a brother: "That's Bill O'Brien. He's head yard inspector on the B & M. All he has to do is ride out with an engineer twice a day and look things over. He gets two hundred a month, he's fixed all right." For pages Williams fumbles, trying to do controlled justice to his admiration for the gardener; trying, more importantly, to take his measure as a person through the remarks of various people who have known him. He is "a tough bird." He is uncomplaining — or at least "I never heard him complain." He is "a character." More extravagantly, he is "worth the whole town." He is proud; he told the doctor's wife, when she fretted over something: "You don't need to tell me lady. You've got no fool working for you today." He is a craftsman; "he did his job well." We will never, however, get a final judgment on the man's worth or his "personality." The doctor himself comes as near as he can when he says, tersely: "The way he walks unbegging." Then, at the end, compelled to write a rare (for this volume) general statement, he offers us a touch of rhetoric, amid yet another admission of contrariness: "He has tasted rare sweets, enjoyed rare occasions; it is my conviction that his life has enhanced the dignity of the human spirit and that the dirt and debasement of it do not matter but are the effects of causes little to the honor or credit of those who made up his daily surroundings."

That man, and one suspects, the others whose lives go to make up the "life" Williams is interested in, resists even the most refined of portraiture — hence, it can be added, cynically, the author's resort to talk about "the dignity of the human spirit," a phrase any politician would find congenial. The best passages in the book are less extravagant; passages in which the author is not carried away with admiration, but intent on getting across a confusing picture; passages in which his social criticism is indirect, or his respect is clearly earned by the outcome of a particular incident, or his anger is most openly expressed, the inevitable response of someone (the doctor) who is himself part of the frustrating confrontation he is describing. Here, for instance, is Williams on upper-class theoreticians who come to "help" the working class "rise," or maybe rise up: "When they had the big strike at the textile mills and that bright boy from Boston came down and went shooting off his mouth around in the streets here telling us what to do: who paid for having their kids and women beat up by the police? Did the guy take a room down on Monroe St. and offer his services for the next ten years at

fifty cents a throw to help straighten up the messes
he helped get us into? He did not. The Polocks
paid for it all. Sure. And raised up sons to be cops
too. I don't blame them. Somebody's got to take the
jobs."

He is quite blunt about the brainy Bostonian, but
the vantage point for the observation is not his,
but that of the working people of Paterson and its
neighboring towns. And always, there is the willingness to accept a much less than perfect world as
one not all that bad, or deserving of unqualified
censure. The Boston social reformer can always
leave; his "purity" of purpose is cushioned by
money and influence. The Polocks are there, forever
there, and simply trying to keep up with the bills,
keep their stomachs full. They do indeed respect
outsiders; Williams would never even hint at it,
but he is one of them. I don't know how much he
charged his Polock patients, but I'd guess that some
paid nothing, not "fifty cents a throw." Moreover,
he maintained his practice in northern New Jersey
for nearer to a half a century, as opposed to ten
years — never, though, falling back on his "services"
as an excuse for being an "expert." Nothing in
Life Along the Passaic River lends itself to any
thesis or position with respect to one or another
"class" of people. One can with equal encouragement from the author stress the wretchedness of
"life" he witnessed, or its unyielding values in the

face of little encouragement indeed. Most of all, though, as Williams upon occasion admitted to himself, the stories he wrote, one after the other, were efforts made in the face of adversity — the hectic, demanding life of a full-time general practitioner. In a sense, then, they were achievements not unlike those managed by others who lived along the Passaic: children cared for and reared, even if with difficulty; gardens rendered lovely; products made and made and made, however little the wages of those who did so.

It is no secret that the man who published these stories in the midst of the Great Depression was no widely hailed and lavishly paid writer. Quite the contrary, he was making very little, if anything, for the words he mustered in between patients or late, late at night; and few were rushing to read those words. Only a stroke — not literary fame or a position at some university — ended his practice, his day-to-day stay among the plain, ordinary people of New Jersey whose knack of survival he couldn't help regarding with a mixture of admiration, sadness, and bitterness. He despaired for the people whose lives he witnessed; given the America of the 1930s, the survival they accomplished seemed almost futile. But he often found himself almost unwittingly surprised and delighted by these people; their words and deeds could prove him needlessly impatient, ungenerous, short-sighted,

and gloomy. Most impressive, he could be relentlessly self-observant and self-critical, even as he
was the writer who appraised others and wrote up
his various impressions.

To its great credit, this book reveals one "bright
boy," this one from New Jersey rather than Massachusetts, as quite able to go back to school and
learn: the college of hard knocks and its curricula —
with classes going on all the time, day or night,
and with a thoroughly "unstructured educational
environment." And like many students who stay
in school for years and years, the book's author
succumbed, finally, to a certain fever: what he kept
learning must be told to others, hopefully in a contagious way, so that they would not easily forget, and
would in turn join a certain community of like-
minded people — perhaps what every writer dreams
of helping to build. The result is that peculiarly
abrasive guile of a certain kind of perennial student
— as if nothing in northern New Jersey could possibly surprise or undo him, and everything in the
region might one day be of possible value in some
test. The tests, of course, become the stories; each
one of them has the doctor faltering or scratching
his head or shouting ouch. He never grades himself, though — never comes across as self-congratulatory or clever or all too accomplished as a witness
and a writer. I suppose he would have been glad
to be told that in what he saw (accurately) and told

(well) he passed, and so could stay precisely where he was and wanted to be, one of "them" who was part of all that "life along the Passaic River," as well as one of "us" whose fate it is to read books and come to conclusions about those who write them and, in this case, those about whom a series of stories were written.

Arguably, all efforts to write about, never mind render abstractions on, the nature of human existence involve an act of violence: the flow of the Passaic is interfered with here, there, and everywhere by the arbitrariness of words, however sensitive, respectful and, it is hoped, appropriate, let alone the grand designs of those who want to stop rivers (all the world, even) with the pretentious bulk of theory and more theory. In "The Use of Force" a doctor contrives casually, then energetically, then desperately to get his spoon down a child's mouth, so that he can examine her. Sick as she obviously was, the struggle had to be fierce; the girl wouldn't surrender. Finally, she is overpowered, and the doctor finds out about her: "She had fought valiantly to keep me from knowing her secret. She had been hiding that sore throat for three days at least and lying to her parents in order to escape just such an outcome as this." Not one to give up without a last-ditch effort, she attacked the doctor, even though he had already moved away, victorious with his vision obtained, his "material" for a slide. In a touching and powerful conclusion, the doctor reminds us that at the point he had, at last, seen what he felt he had an obligation to see, "tears of defeat blinded her [the girl's] eyes." One who refuses to forget such a confrontation is unlikely to expect too much of himself: there is simply no evading the costs of interference, whatever the gain — and words, Williams always knew, have their own "force." Still, the girl was, he tells us at the start, "as strong as a heifer in appearance," so there was every likelihood that she would recover, even as her doctor's stories show not the least sign of wear and tear, of lessened value as a particular mode of entry to Paterson's working-class life,[5] for all the nearly four decades of their life.

Part Two

Arrival in America

Arrival in America

In *I Wanted to Write a Poem* (1958), William Carlos Williams looked back to his state of mind in the 1930s. He described himself as "obsessed by the plight of the poor." He was frank to say how he wrote the stories that made up *Life Along the Passaic River:* "The best stories were written at white heat. I would come home from my practice and sit down and write until the story was finished, ten to twelve pages. I seldom revised at all." He not only depended upon his medical practice for the plots to those stories, but drew literally and with apology upon the words of his patients. He was in love with their way of putting things. He regarded their talk as blunt, lively, honest, and right to the point. In his *Autobiography* he recalls a college English instructor asking him: "But this language of yours, where does it come from?" The reply: "From the mouths of Polish mothers." He attended more than Polish mothers, as the stories demonstrate. And those mothers provided him with more

than a fresh, vital language; they alerted him to
their strivings, ambitions and disappointments —
as women who were trying hard to bring up their
children, often in the face of severe hardship. Even
as Williams was writing the Passaic stories he had
conceived of a novel and was for years, in the 1920s
and 1930s, working at it intermittently, but with
great concern if not passion. *White Mule* was published eight months before *Life Along the Passaic
River,* through readers of *Pagany* and *The Maga-
zine* had seen chapters of it long before. For the
novel, Dr. Williams also drew from his clinical
work, as he makes clear in *I Wanted to Write a
Poem:* "After all I was a physician and not only that
I was a pediatrician and I'd always wanted to write
a book about a baby." He describes himself, a little
later on, as "filled up with babies," the result of
years of work in New York City (at Postgraduate
Hospital and Babies Hospital) as well as in northern
New Jersey. But he was, in addition, the husband of
a woman who had borne him two sons, and she, in
turn, was the daughter of a man whose life, with
all its drama and struggles, had quite strongly
caught the imagination of his son-in-law.

White Mule is many things — for one, an account
of Mrs. Williams' childhood, from the moment
of her birth on, as the second daughter of a man
given the fictional name Joe Stecher, a Silesian
immigrant to New York City in the latter part of the

nineteenth century, and his wife Gurlie, a restless, ambitious and troubled Norwegian immigrant who surely "rode" her husband much more than Dr. Williams' beloved Floss is described by the author as doing to him: "What should I call the book? Then it came to me: *White Mule*. Floss, I knew, was a mule. And she was white. There was another meaning. At that time, during the Depression, we were drinking White Mule. Floss was like a shot of whiskey to me—her disposition cantankerous, like all wives, riding her man for his own good whether he liked it or not." It is an interesting remark—a bit mysterious, and like any writer's "explanation" of the sources of his inspiration, risky to interpret. Williams was rather comfortable with his "creativity" (an awful, self-important word, but then, no substitute word can really work); he was quite willing to be a mule to himself, and as for "white," he has described his passion for writing as a "white heat." In any event, the novel turned out to be the first of three, and the trilogy turned out to be yet another attempt on Williams' part to suggest the quality of a rather broad arc of American life — with respect to time, from the 1890s to the 1920s, and with respect to people and place, the heterogeneous, confusing, volatile life of New York City's nineteenth and early twentieth century immigrants.

White Mule is an extraordinary psychological

novel; or rather, a novel that uses, among other de-
vices, an infant's insistent presence, and later on, a
child's growing awareness, as a means of acquaint-
ing the reader with a whole range of feelings and
shifts of feeling, all of which the author aims to
represent and comprehend. Freud was pleased
when Thomas Mann and others in the literary world
acknowledged how helpful, but also challenging,
his discoveries were: they enabled us to understand more explicitly mental life, and might enable
(given genuine talent in a writer, as opposed to a
faddish interest in the "application" of psychological ideas to story-telling) an increasing complexity
and subtlety to a future generation of novelists. I
would imagine that Anna Freud, who almost single-
handedly developed the field of child psychoanalysis, might similarly respond to *White Mule,* which
is, however, no heavy-handed tract on child development, but does give a child's earliest years —
the expanding physical and psychological capaci-
ties of Flossie — both a chronological and symbolic
role in the novel: chronological, because the novel
opens with Flossie's birth, and through the trilogy
we more or less follow her enlarging life; and symbolic, because she is an American-born child whose
experience — her complex inheritance from Europe,
her urban childhood, her increasing familiarity
with suburban and rural life — it is the novelist's
intention to examine broadly enough so that the

rest of us may learn something about ourselves and our nation.

The Victorian novel had its fair share of death scenes — long, elaborate, full of significance. Even now a good novelist can use such a scene to great advantage: in Walker Percy's *The Last Gentleman*, the extended death of a youth is an occasion for all sorts of philosophical exposition — done without heavy hand by a novelist who has read (and re-read) contemporary existentialist writers like Marcel and Heidegger. Williams knew, as both an obstetrician and pediatrician, that a child's birth can not only be an occasion of expectation, joy, and fulfillment, but a time of great upheaval — for the mother, who may visualize all too clearly the tasks and responsibilities ahead, or the father, who may also realize what faces him, at the very minimum as a breadwinner, but also for both of them as individuals: citizens of a nation, members of a certain family, inhabitants of an apartment or a house in such-and-such a location. "To Be," Williams calls the first chapter of *White Mule*, and no doubt about it, there is a brilliant description of Flossie's birth and first moments — done exactly right by someone who knew to the last detail what happens at such a time. But rather quickly on we begin to realize that the "To Be" refers not only to Flossie, but her parents, who are themselves, it can be said, struggling to be born: to find a place for themselves in

a new and confusing country, to find a way of life
that satisfies, and not least, appeases various yearn-
ings and mandates if not outright obsessions. Williams is wonderfully responsive to the temperament of Gurlie Stecher, whose intense desire for a
son, and consequent disappointment upon the occasion of Flossie's birth, emerges as, ironically,
more a reflection of a person's social, political, and
economic situation than an indication of a "deep,"
or as we put it, a psychodynamic conflict. To have
resisted the narrow, psychological reductionism of
the 1920s and 1930s is a minor but noteworthy
achievement of the author's.

Williams had no particular interest in psychiatry,
but he knew that the city Paterson lived in each of
its inhabitants. The poem *Paterson* contains an
inseparable mixture of "interior" monologue and
"exterior" social reportage or analysis, along with
historical comment. By the same token, Williams
makes Flossie's birth both particular and a part of
something else—she was born of a given mother,
but also at a given moment in the history of medicine and American society. There is, to my knowledge, nothing like Williams' account of Flossie's
encounter with the world: "The air enclosed her,
she felt it all over her, touching, waking her. . . .
Screwing up her tiny smeared face, she let out three
convulsive yells—and lay still." Yet, we are quickly
asked to shift our attention, however entranced by

the writer's skill at handling an unusual subject: "Stop that crying, said Mrs. D, you should be glad to get outa that hole." A midwife is speaking, and we are in a New York tenement. The father is at the door, a step or two from his wife — and immediately able to hear her frank remark: "But I wanted a boy." No doctor intimidates her; nor a hospital, with its rituals and demands. No modern sensibility, either: one is outspoken only on certain subjects. Gurlie never would have talked about sex as candidly as we do. But she could insist that Mrs. D her midwife "look again," and when told once more (she had no anaesthesia in her) that yes, it *was* a girl, she could say: "Take it away. I don't want it." I don't question that such an attitude is still to be found; but I doubt that today such a direct assertion is likely, even from those least inhibited by American customs and values. I am thinking of some of the Chicano women I have come to know in the Rio Grande Valley of Texas or in New Mexico. They belong to a "culture" well known for its emphasis on *machismo*. Many of them do indeed pride themselves on the sons they have brought into their family, their *husband's* family. But they, too, are Americans, alive in this last quarter, virtually, of the twentieth century. So, one can hear this in Truchas, New Mexico: "I had a girl last week. I was glad. I mean, my husband would have wanted a son; and me, too. But still, I was glad. Even if you are disappointed, you can be very happy."

No such mixture for Gurlie. She was not merely disappointed; she was belligerent—utterly out-raged by yet another blow of fate. As we will learn repeatedly from her, she comes from a family that once upon a time (those last four words have so often been on the lips of immigrants) prospered in the old country. But now she is in noisy, crowded New York, and married to Joe Stecher, who is a printer, who seems maddeningly satisfied with things as they are—or if not, quite unwilling to be as dissatisfied as she is. So, "to be" is no easy matter, not for the newborn child, and certainly not for her parents. Williams is wonderfully ironic, and not in the least self-consciously didactic as a writer who has some ideas about what we might call "the determinants of child development," when he juxtaposes the following two paragraphs:

In prehistoric ooze it lay while Mrs. D wound the white twine about its pale blue stem with kindly clumsy knuckles and blunt fingers with black nails and with the wiped-off scissors from the cord at her waist, cut it—while it was twisting and flinging up its toes and fingers into the way—free.

Alone it lay upon its back on the bed, sagging down in the middle by the smeared triple mountain of its mother's disgusted thighs and toppled belly.

Free at last—but not at all free; or, one might
say, free to be under the shadow of that "triple
mountain." And then, there is Mrs. D, a midwife
and practical nurse, who can speak sentimentally,
philosophically, with proper piety—a person whose
words the author can use to contrast the desires of
the infant's mother with those conventionally up-
held. "It is a hard thing to be born a girl," Mrs. D
says as she approaches Flossie with kindness and
consideration. "In the folds of the groin," we learn,
"the crotch where the genitals all bulging and angry
red seemed presages of some future growth, she
rubbed the warm oil, carefully—for she was a good
woman—and thoroughly, cleaning her fingers on
her apron. She parted the little parts looking and
wondering at their smallness and perfection and
shaking her head forebodingly." Gurlie doesn't
have to be told why Mrs. D shook her head with
that kind of feeling. Gurlie knew better than to
show pity, or to acknowledge feeling apprehensive.
Gurlie had long since decided that in America one
wins or one loses; by definition, alas, Mrs. D had
gone as far as she ever would: a person who attends
others. Not that fate for Gurlie, and not for her
older daughter Lottie, and not for this new-born
Flossie. For Gurlie love—the best kind of love any
infant could receive—ought to be the kind that day
in, day out, works against Mrs. D's complacent if

generous pietism; and too, works against the infant's inevitable, unwitting passivity: "The body lay back at ease with closed eyes — lolling about as it was lifted by a leg, an arm, and turned."

Williams is as determined with Gurlie as he was with the doctor who treated the woman with "a face of stone." To the latter he was gruff, to the point, almost, of implausibility; even *prejudiced* doctors (and they are, one presumes, not unknown) don't quite admit to themselves, let alone their patients, how antagonistic they happen to feel toward, say, factory workers. In *White Mule*, as well, conventional sentiment (personified by the midwife) meets up with an almost brutal candor — and of a kind that does not slowly go away as the infant grows. The midwife is protective; she won't press "the spot in the top of the head," in hopes that she will thereby get the baby to stop crying. It is "a cruel thing to do." She washes, cleans, oils the infant, hovers over it, engages nicely with its father, whose tenderness and concern are quite apparent. For the mother, however, the arrival of the girl is not only a cause for disappointment, but "disgust and anger," and even "fury." At one point, as mentioned, she demands, point blank: "Take it away and let me rest." The nurse thinks, maybe says, "God pardon you for saying that." Williams does not use quotation marks anywhere in the novel, a brilliant strategy: we occasionally don't quite know what is on the person's mind, what is suggested or revealed by gesture, grimace, or glare, and what is actually spoken. One can picture the midwife raising an eyebrow, averting her gaze, or even opening her mouth in surprised disapproval, but speaking nothing of what she thinks. At times, of course, Williams is explicit about matters: "You miserable scrawny little brat, she thought. . . ."

Williams knew infants intimately; it is not simply the drama of birth he is content to provide us. There are careful, beautifully rendered descriptions of the infant's life: how it takes (and rejects) food, from its mother's breasts and from the nurse who, alas, will be around for a rather brief spell; and how it asserts itself—reddens, sobs, cries long and hard, to the point that the notion of a "helpless infant" gradually strikes the reader as untenable. By the time we come across the sentence "but now, the baby began to rebel," we need no lectures from Melanie Klein [1] to the effect that a newborn baby has various "attitudes," states of mind—something more complicated, more *psychological*, than mere reflexes. Williams has shown that the way one handles an infant has a rather quick, noticeable, and important bearing on the child's mind as well as its spinal column. In three sentences he manages to evoke the purposive as well as responsive side of an infant's mental life quite well—the equal, certainly, of chapters in any text of "child development":

It sobbed and forced its piercing little voice so small
yet so disturbing in its penetrating puniness, mastering
its whole surroundings till it seemed to madden them. It
caught its breath and yelled in sobs and long shrill
waves. It sobbed and squeezed its yell into their ears.

Their ears, Gurlie's and Joe's, had other (it turns
out, competing) demands to contend with, some of
them, also, quite noisy. The time was April of 1893;
and as the author makes clear, Joe was not living in
Silesia, at the foot of snowy mountains and near
fields newly covered with spring flowers. He and
his family occupied a flat on 104th Street in Manhattan—four flights up a brownstone, with an elevated nearby. There was a park within walking
distance, but who can sit in it and forget all that
surrounded it—this country? Even so, Williams can
briefly be a nature poet, for all the limitations of a
small urban park: "The grass was soaked with dew,
the benches were too wet to sit on. But the sun
blazed in the washed air." Then he does a quick
about-face, through Joe: "America, he thought as
he sauntered, the United States of America—
money. Without money, nothing. Money." It is
the beginning of a long meditation; a workingman,
an immigrant, a man just become a father for the
second time, tries to make sense of his various
loyalties and convictions. He fails, though he never
comes to the conclusion that he has. How many of
us do? How many of us are so consistent in the

values we uphold, in the choices we make, that we
are never tempted to strike out at various individuals, or more collectively, at one or another
"group," as a means of letting ourselves off the
various hooks our own minds feel compelled to put
us on (a matter of emotional desperation that has
nothing to do with logic or education)? It is a delicately wrought fabric of thought which Williams
seems almost effortlessly able to let fall on (rather
than force upon) one of his principal characters.
The point of departure, one can say, the givens
which Joe must reluctantly but decisively bid
good-bye, are the high principles he learned as a
child: Christ's teachings and a kind of goodwill and
moral earnestness which need no religious sanction
—merely a new parent's natural hope for his own
children that life will be good and fair. "Men who
work should have enough money," he declares to
himself. Nor by that does he mean to be exclusive:
only those of us who do, in fact, have work ought
to be lucky enough to have money—and let those
who for one reason or another don't or can't or won't
find work pay the severe penalty of being penniless. "Everybody should work," he says. The only
qualification is this: "Everybody should work the
best he knows how."

Joe has worked himself, always and gladly and
conscientiously. Not only was he a printer; he had
stood alongside Gompers and Hilyard—as, in fact,

Dr. Williams' father-in-law had, and helped establish *The Workers' Journal.* Karl Marx would not object to Joe's aspirations for his fellow man: from each according to his abilities, to each according to his needs. There is, at first, no impulse in Joe to rush to the defense of capitalists, or modify his hopes for himself and others like him out of "economic realism." For a while Joe is too realistic himself to defend the status quo on the basis of "realism"; on the basis of his own self-interest he does so later — gradually, begrudgingly, with great pain and not a little sadness. One can even argue, calling upon the titles of book two and three of the trilogy, that the whole point of these novels is to indicate, with the degree of subtlety and refinement necessary, how long it takes, how many illusions, self-deceptions, rationalizations and on and on, are required, before a man gets what turn out to be the demons of intelligence and good conscience off his back, so that he is uninterruptedly free — not "to be," as Flossie was declared in the first chapter of *White Mule,* but to plow ahead in America.

Williams summons that image of plowing, of cutting up and cleaving through, on the last page of *The Build-Up,* when he has Joe tell an architect to dig ahead, no matter the cost, and whatever the impediments, so that he and Gurlie will have their "big stone house of native-cut stone." The immigrant will become a native, an American, at all costs: "No matter. Blast! Blast it out!" he says. "We're going to have a house like nothing in the neighborhood. Like nothing." In plain view, of course, is someone else's home — "the mansion of the tycoon on the mountain." Even among the very rich, the rich who make a successful Joe seem middle class indeed, there are challenges, frustrations, limits that seem unyielding — and always, competition, with the inevitable accompaniment of envy and rivalry. But Williams knows that only in novels, or rarely, in the careers of confidence men or individuals visited by exceptional luck, does money get "built-up" overnight. It takes not only time, but a developing willingness to position oneself and gain control over one's vocabulary; that is, to step here, move there, say this, keep silent about that. One has to forget as well as remember; push aside in one's mind old, bothersome "lessons" or beliefs, and keep up front a certain readiness — not only for action, but for self-justification.

Maybe the mind is agile and quick to adjust; maybe those who write novels like *The Rise of Silas Lapham,* or, with respect to immigrants, *The Rise of David Levinsky,* make too much of the accommodations, the maneuvers and pretenses involved in personal and social "advancement." Williams knows, however, that even crooks at some "level" have to live with, or fight off, various images and sentiments, if not what some of us, a bit self-importantly, refer to as "ideas" or "values." His novels have correctly been described as Flaubertian. Vivienne Koch [2] declares him anxious "to reveal what he sees without comment, to record not only what he *should* observe, but what he does observe." She adds: "He is especially anxious to eliminate the 'I,' to write as if from another world." She refers to a "genuine desire" on Williams' part, "to annihilate the 'self.'" "In *White Mule*," she goes on to point out, "Williams begins with society." And, drawing on John Crowe Ransom's alternatives of "structure" and "texture," she asserts that "sometimes, in fact, *White Mule* seems all texture." Neither she, nor of course Ransom himself, necessarily attach any pejorative or preferential implication to those words; it all depends, obviously, on the particular artist and what he or she does or does not achieve. But I wonder whether those formulations or categorizations quite work, however helpful or suggestive it is to have a simplification (a word which I hope I myself use without pejorative intent).

There is certainly more than the "texture" of society in the chain of thoughts Joe has as he leaves his tenement house, walks along New York's crowded streets, purchases his paper, and continues under the elevated toward the park, in Williams' word, "pondering." Joe's "self" is not merely revealed by the way he acts, the various social "roles" he fits into (well or not-so-well): husband, father, worker, hesitant (at first) but (in the end) fiercely determined entrepreneur, American citizen, immigrant from Germany, New Yorker, suburbanite, owner of a country place. Joe also thinks a lot; his mind wanders and tries to make sense of what he sees and is trying to accomplish at home and in the office of a printing company. The "structure" of his mind, it can be said, or, put differently, the essence of his "self" (both psychodynamic, ethical, and, even, spiritual) comes across in a number of "interior" passages, which, it can be maintained, represent more than a casual device on the author's part, a break in his preoccupation with texture — but rather the very objective he has: to show how ultimately, at certain important moments in our lives, the mind actively strives to make a pattern of the various social and emotional threads that get called a "life." Speaking of "lives" and a "life," one is struck, as one reads Joe's reflections in the second chapter, and again, in the next to the last chapter (XXI) of *White Mule*, how adroitly and sensibly the author has made use of all that he observed among northern New Jersey's working-class people and too, the state's upper-middle-class people. In his own manner he immersed himself in others; he wasn't around "recording" people, taping their words or writing comments furtively after they had spoken, but, rather, engaging with them directly, delivering their children, caring for their health, responding to them, as doctors used to do quite naturally, and even today occasionally do.

The cast of Joe Stecher's mind in the second chapter is that of a man who can't seem to distinguish his own, personal struggles from those of America's. Williams connects the abstract (labor unions, politicians and their easy corruptibility, the needs of the poor, the rights of those who have worked hard and want to hold on to what they have earned) with the concrete: Joe as a particular person, whose childhood still weighs heavy on him, whatever the distance from it he has come in space and time. In Germany he had been a bright, studious lad. His father had died, though, when he was a youth, and he had to assume many family obligations: "But he had to work, to get money quick — brother to the music conservatory, sisters to America, mother to keep." There is, therefore, a heritage, and a fate — both brought to this country. If things had been different, if his father had not died, if Germany's economic life had been more sustaining — those ifs never quite leave Joe's mind, at least for good. They are an inheritance which a few robins in a small Harlem park quite readily summon — as does the arrival of a newborn, whose American childhood will not be what her father may have once imagined for his future children when he was young and in Europe. Robins in New York are not

pheasants in a German forest. But there are connections that make America seem not all that different,
but simply another version of what was quite familiar in Silesia or Berlin; to call upon the words of a
book's title as a summary of those connections: *The
Protestant Ethic and the Spirit of Capitalism* — the
author of which, incidentally, also was a German.
"In Berlin men worked," Joe recalls. Then he
makes a contrast: "Here they had strikes — to get
more money." But he knows that without money in
this world (of America or Germany then, of America
or Germany later, as he grows older) one is utterly
lost, at the mercy of everyone's power, contempt,
willfulness, or Christian charity, the last thoroughly
scarce, as Joe knows. The Protestant ethic *becomes*
the spirit of capitalism; work becomes a god, *the*
god. Joe went to church "fairly regularly," but
Sunday had become for him, as for others, not a
day set aside for prayer, but a strange, unsettling
interruption — it makes one feel like "a machine
that is broken."

Williams is by no means completely able to keep
himself out of the narrative. He lets us know that
Joe is "bitterly confused"; the author is not, however, gratuitously telling the obvious when he says
that. He has done a good job of connecting up the
various confusions Joe struggles with — to the point
that his lapses of logic are so familiar to all of us,
we are inclined to overlook them, lest we be made

too uncomfortable ourselves. Who doesn't believe in a fair day's pay for a fair day of work—that is, who among those many who are proud to distinguish themselves as Americans? True, he has his nostalgia, his yearning for the Black Forest, maybe—he would be a head forester, an *ober förster,* he thinks to himself, using for emphasis the German word; but over and over again the powerful reality of America intrudes upon his consciousness: "There it was again—America," he says at one point. Then come the awful details: "It rose in his clear mind as something beyond the grasp of reason, something medieval, ignorant, arrogant—at once rich and cheap." Even worse, he sees the struggle facing him in this country as utterly demeaning and corrupting: "A battle for something without value at the cost of all he knew of that was worthwhile." What indeed had he been trained to believe in? He becomes vague in his mind, as pietistic as any number of ministers he no doubt never really heard, only endured: "Material honesty, a logic of work and pay." With that brief answer of Joe's, is the novelist forcing things a bit, all too apparently intruding on the thoughts and ruminations (the "associations" some of us feel disposed to call them) of a principal character of his?

In Lynn, Massachusetts, at the height of the Vietnam War, and the protests which accompanied it, I heard an American factory worker, an employee of General Electric rather than a small printing company, speak of what it meant for him, as the son of an Italian immigrant, to be "living well," he kept insisting, in America. For him, though, as for Joe Stecher, America is a paradox. To get at this paradox, to make an effort at least, at undermining the "bitterly confused" rush of feelings he sensed in himself, the man would call upon phrases, whole sentences, sometimes, he'd lifted out of sermons, radio and television commercials, newspaper articles, and God alone knows where else: "This is the greatest land on earth. There's justice here; you keep yourself law-abiding, and stay within the Constitution, you know, and there are the privileges of being free. If you don't, then it's not your country; you should go elsewhere. I believe we ought to preserve our freedoms. We have a noble heritage. There are enemies who want to destroy us. But God can't bless America, unless each and every one of us helps out. Otherwise you're on the road to Communism, something bad like that. I wish these college people, who always are on the back of this country, knocking it, would read the Bill of Rights and the Declaration of Independence and the Constitution—they are what make America so great. There's a lot that's no good here; I remember my father talking about the old country. Here it's kill or be killed. Here every politician is out for himself. And those businessmen, do they fleece you! More

and more! But you've got to make the best of things.
I take an Alka-Seltzer when a lot of these troubles
in the world get to me! At least I've got my health,
though! It's *not* everything; I don't agree with
that. (Not when you have bills you can't pay.) But
it's a lot."

Not much different from "material honesty" and
the "logic of work and pay." Joe smiles as he talks
to himself: "I am an American after all," he says.
But what is an American for him, for the American
I have just quoted (an Italian-American factory
worker who is a Catholic New Englander, and who,
unlike a cousin of his now living in Toledo, Ohio,
loves the shore, and so on), for each of us, with our
peculiar and shared memories, ideals, expectations?
Joe believes that he is affirming his American nature "after all" when he declares himself not especially wicked or crafty or greedy, simply intelligent
and adventurous. He has thought of a way, through
the machine, to do "something requiring accuracy
and everlasting care." He has thought of a way of
doing something rare if not unique. He is delighted
with himself—but soon enough troubled. Immediately after concluding that he is "an American after
all" he adds this qualification: "Not a grafter, though.
I'll give them work if they'll pay a fair price for it.
Work that is work. A good price." And a second or
two later: "Money, money, money—whether you
want to or not you've got to think about it." That

imperative comes to mind after he has reminded himself that he is now the father of two children — one man's blunt realization that if his daughter was going "to be," it would be necessary for him to risk becoming less in his own estimation.

On the one hand he is getting obsessed with money; on the other hand he is enraged by those who urge strikes, who practice a "business of holding up the game to get a rake off from it." It is a practice which "affronted his philosophy"; it is a practice which is "foreign to his nature"; it is a practice which "he did not understand." But he understands something; his nature is not all that incompatible with commercial life; his philosophy is less vulnerable to self-inflicted criticism than he believes. Faced with contradictions, he strikes out: "It's the Irish, he thought to himself, and the Sheenies. Those are the suckers who spoil everything. They don't like good work. Money, that's all, money."

No doubt J. P. Morgan and others like him — the Mr. Lemon, for example, to whose club Joe goes when he is getting ready to accept financial backing for his own venture into business — would not be too chagrined by such a line of thought. Even the rich and mighty have to struggle with words, with the sayings they learned in school ("might doesn't make right," or does it?), with all those sermons on all those Sundays, delivered by ministers who know whom to smile broadly at, whom to go ask for help. "Bricks for Christ," a sign asked for, not far from the home of the Italian-American mentioned earlier; and the church is Catholic, presumably a touch removed from the long-standing influence of homespun American pieties. Mr. Lemon is not at all unhappy to have his club; the rabble can be kept out. Best for him, however, and for Joe when he joins such a club, that the rabble be available and noticeable — and in a pinch, conjured up. Otherwise, one would have to acknowledge the exclusion of just plain ordinary people, whose everyday dedication and honesty would seem to merit membership in any organization. Dr. Williams is not so trite as to have Joe stare long and hard in the mirror, then smash it. Better a baseball game, where he can see men hitting, running, shouting, jeering, plotting, heckling — all in the game. The nearer he gets to that game, the closer he looks at it, the more complicated, the more vexing, the more contrived, and potentially sly or dishonest everyone or everything seems: "A little self-consciously he wandered toward the pitcher's mound. He hadn't realized how much raised it was above the rest of the diamond. That's just it, he said, when you really get up close to a thing. And the way they whip that ball in!"

He wonders about the apparently casual elegance of the game he had watched, the seeming moral equity: a man throwing a ball, and a man trying to take aim and hit it. He will soon enough be "in the money"; while watching the game he mulls over the details of an arrangement which will launch him toward "a small place in the suburbs, not too far from the city—with a green, well-kept lawn. Flowers, a few trees about it." Then the German word again: *Ein Obstgarten.* It is all in his head, the details of how one lives if one has become well-to-do—the trees, the lawn, the sense of beauty that in turn depends upon someone's successful encounter with the ugliness of commercial life. The baseball players are not only good sports who love to hit, catch, run, but men whose determination to win, to beat others, and the bigger the margin the better, reflects for thousands of viewers the essence of their daily lives. Williams doesn't hammer the theme home; he isn't interested in regarding baseball as a convenient, all-purpose symbol for capitalist competitiveness, the mix of apparent civilization and murderous greed that one can manage to ignore if one works hard at not looking very hard. For Conrad the African jungles provided a way of getting at the "heart" of the comfortable European bourgeoisie's refined drawing rooms. Williams is content with a baseball game; his effort is less ambitious—no extended metaphor—and the object of illumination is, perhaps, less the economic system itself, as revealed through its imperialist under-

belly, than the current of hysteria many of us feel,
the price of our accommodation to that system,
which for us is "the world we live in." So, it is
"Rush, rush, rush!" for Joe, as well as for all those
fans who may not get as far as he will, but at least
can have (hopefully) a few hours of triumph.

Even as Joe is preparing to win his important
game, he hesitates: "But is it worth it?" he asks.
Many of us ask such questions upon occasion; but,
of course, we are "realistic," so we don't really
answer ourselves, simply go on. What choices do
we have? And if told that there *is* a choice — rebel,
or withdraw, or, at the very least, protest loud and
clear — we are quick to reply: and what about the
wife, and the children? Joe never explicitly comes
up with that rejoinder; like many of us, he manages
to stop short of the need for any kind of reply. He
shrugs his shoulders and goes along with the drift
of his life. Accordingly, the chapter which follows
his meditative attendance at a baseball game offers
us a rather idyllic scene in Vermont. Gurlie and her
children have escaped New York tenement life; and
if there are disadvantages — no screens on the windows and plenty of flies and mosquitoes — there are
many, obvious reasons for the mother and her two
daughters to rejoice. Gurlie, within limits, relaxes.
Flossie is by now a toddler; she stands at her
mother's knee and is much stronger than had been
the case a few months earlier. In the country her

never very affectionate mother could at last recognize that "the thing was really beginning to be
attractive."

Not that she ever really lets her guard down completely, this city person, who has always been anxious to extol the simple virtues of rural living to her
husband as a means of goading him to make more
money and thereby enable that possibility. At one
point we are told that "Gurlie was looking at the
chairs and the dishes on the shelf to see if there
was anything old there but she couldn't detect a
thing of value." She also is frustrated with the
Ferrys, her Vermont neighbors: how do they manage to get by? What do they do—with themselves,
with time, with the energy and ambition they *surely*
must possess? (Don't all people?) She never gets
rude. She never dwells on her own questions. Unlike her husband, she is not given to taking those
questions seriously. The answer to them is life
itself: one must move on, move up, get to Vermont,
get to the suburbs, go even beyond them, too, if
at all possible. When Gurlie asks Mrs. Ferry "What
do you do in winter?" there is, perhaps, a touch of
incredulity in her voice, but not the envy she often
claimed to have, in the abstract, while living in New
York, and haranguing her husband on the virtues of
the rustic. That particular inclination of hers, to
badger Joe, is handled by the author rather interestingly. Gurlie never becomes a shrew, one of

Strindberg's amazons. Nor is she a more restrained
nag. She never really spends much time arguing out
her position, or trying to impose it on her husband.
Her appeal to him (and it is that, rather than a
demand) is not unlike the self-justification a successful man can rather easily call upon — after he
has climbed over God knows how many other
people: I'm intelligent, perceptive, hardworking,
conscientious, a born craftsman, and, beyond question, a man of energy and competence; that being
the case, ought I not use my abilities, and ought
they not, in turn, be rewarded by the social and
economic system, for what they contribute — a benefit for everyone, not just me?

Unfortunately, Joe can't quite fully accept that
philosophical position, hence the Irish and Sheenies
he notices and uses for his own purposes. Gurlie
need only look to her children when any vague
unrest comes upon her: don't they deserve better?
And she proves something to herself: when things
do indeed improve, when Flossie's face is "smeared
with berry juice, her hands quite sooty, quite part
of it all," Gurlie is quite clearly a more relaxed,
appealing mother and person. The child has become a "part" of a world Gurlie likes, has coveted
— and all the better for the child as well as the
mother. This gradual psychological change in
Gurlie's "nature" turns out to be of decisive im-

portance; it is a change rendered with great deli-
cacy, and is a stroke of genius on Williams' part.
Gurlie at first is almost too much — at least for those
relatively well-off readers who, most likely, have
and will be the readers of *White Mule*. She is brutally
insistent with her husband, and just as brutally
indifferent, it seems, with Flossie. She can't sat-
isfactorily breast-feed the child, and of course in
this century, even were she to profess her love for
Flossie every hour, any number of us psychologically sophisticated (maybe too sophisticated) readers would be quite ready with our "interpretations."

But Williams needs the tension in the novel
between husband and wife, as well as mother and
child; that way he can provide psychological as
well as social "texture," if not a stretch or two of
"structure": the "dynamics of family life," in today's
not especially attractive language. Not that he wants
to caricature Gurlie; she is no more fixed in "personality" or character than Flossie. She is, really,
a woman of her word; she can indeed be appeased,
even if at the start of the trilogy her price seems
high — nothing less than a quick rise up the social
scale. And she loves her husband; she never says
so, but we can feel it in the passion of her avowal of
his possibilities, however mixed with coarse and
rude coaxing: "In America bluff is everything. You
say that all the time. Then be a bluff, be a better

bluff than they are. You know you are better than they are. You know you are the best trained printer in America today."

For one thing, her husband has already granted her, repeatedly, her main premise. Her task, as she feels it rather than sees it, is not to prompt insights in an obtuse or ideologically reluctant man. They basically agree — and with them, ideologically, stood (and stand) millions who will never move out of tenements (or the small bungalows of "street-car suburbs") to the grander life of what the English might call the countrified suburbs. The issue is action: will such an eminently able man fire himself up and plunge into the caldron which the American melting pot contains, or will he sit back and obey orders while others fight it out for money and power? As she pushes, demands, cajoles, entices with flattery, which at the same time she earnestly means, he begs off, becomes annoyed, tells her to shut up, but also becomes "somehow excited." Maybe, he wonders, her fiery petulance and outspoken ambitiousness have to do with the recent pregnancy; she was "no longer carrying a baby," and was going through a psychological transition of sorts. Nevertheless, he was not only "understanding," in the patronizing way the word is sometimes used; he "felt admiration" for her. Her contagious willfulness became his through a psychological osmosis Williams knows better than to spell out in full and presumptuous mechanistic detail. We get, instead, a marvelously brief but suggestive phrase: "A borrowed resentment against the world momentarily possessed him."

Not "momentarily," it turns out. There is a Greek chorus of "yes, she was right" in his mind as he takes over where his wife has left off. She has spoken in personal terms; he was better than most, and he ought play his hand accordingly — bluff, take every risk, stay with things in order to come out the winner. As for herself, she was now the mother of two daughters, she reminded him, but beyond that she wanted to insist (quite honestly) upon her sense of herself: "I am not going to sit down and be a *hausfrau*. I am going to live and see the world, and I must have money. And you are going to make it for me." When she spoke those words, he had told her to stop such talk. But later, after her spirit had worked its way into him, he struggles to come to terms with the implication of her apparently self-centered description of what life ought to be like for her. After all, she is going to "live" and "see the world," but she is quite content to judge millions of others worthy of no "life" at all, and no exposure to the world's beautiful side. Gurlie can be both indifferent to or contemptuous of those "others." Actually, she dismisses virtually everyone but her husband, and is perfectly willing to have him step over anyone on his way up.

But he is not so callous. Or shall we, more delicately, call him less stubborn or "aggressive"? He is the one who will be doing the stepping (and calculating, if not plotting); and he is no confidence man. He has a conscience. He cares about his family, but he also prizes his work for what it means to others as well as for what it gets, and might get, for himself. If he is to unleash himself, he has to leave the company of his fellow workers psychologically before he can set about trying to accomplish what his wife asks of him rhetorically and without specification. As soon as he can acknowledge with confidence that Gurlie is right, that he is indeed "abler than the rest," he is free to turn from a part of his own nature, abandon some of his values, and self-righteously rebuff his neighbors and co-workers: "Give those bums something to do and they botch it every time." A rather unqualified description—followed by another one, just in case any part of him has any lingering doubts: "Not one, scarcely, can do the simplest thing without making a mess of it." Then he grants them this: "But they want the money!"

A good deal has been written by psychiatrists about "the psychology of leadership." We are told that the leader becomes, in his person, a kind of focus for the projected strivings and aspirations of his followers; and that he becomes a "super-ego figure," whose advocacy of certain positions reso-

nates with the sense of what ought to be which thousands or millions, as the case may be, feel "deep
down," a consequence of their upbringing. But
what of our business leaders? They are, it seems,
a different sort—by no means universally admired,
and often, alas, quite unknown, even to stockhold-
ers, who, one might assume, have a vested interest
in keeping abreast of who runs this or that corpora-
tion. And why the lack of analysis of such "leadership" by our psychiatrists—not always unwilling to
take on for "analysis" individuals they have little
or no direct access to? What prompts a person to go
after money and more money—to leave the ranks, so
to speak—to keep doing so, even when he or she
appears to be floating in cash and possessions, as
compared to what he or she once had or to what
most people will ever have in the course of their
lives?

Gurlie singles out her husband as the very best;
she draws upon an entire nation for comparison.
And he isn't really in disagreement with her. Even
when she is most critical of him she accuses him
not of modesty, never mind self-loathing. He is
"too careful"; he has "no daring"; he hasn't learned
how to "bluff." Somehow he must rise and rise,
become for others a boss if not a leader. Williams
makes it quite clear that Flossie's birth is the occasion not only for Gurlie to become more absolute
and articulate in her demands, but for Joe to assert

himself—and keep doing so. Without in the least becoming "psychological," Williams indicates to us that for a man like Joe to abandon a previous camaraderie with others (the labor union as protector of all) in favor of a battle to be waged on his own behalf exclusively, requires more than an author's manipulativeness. Plot can account for what Joe does, and what in turn happens to him. Social "texture" can tell us what his deeds will become part of—a particular world, either beckoning or frustrating. But first come those twists and turns of the mind, which this novelist neither wants to play up or down. He won't devote pages to Joe's reveries; they are always responsive to the speech of others, to an event (the baseball game) that takes place around him, and, as a result, they are far more "true to life" and penetrating than an extended "stream-of-consciousness" technique can permit.

I believe that in the name of "depth" the "stream-of-consciousness" novelistic technique offers a distorted, even false, entry into the human mind at work. True, it seems to provide a literary parallel to the analysand's five-day-a-week experience: associations and more associations—with the analyst (and in the case of the novel, the reader or literary critic) left to interpret what has been said spontaneously. But how spontaneously are the associations of even a patient whose analyst is avowedly "neutral," and more or less silent most of the time?

Psychiatrists ought to know (though certainly some
of us tend to forget or overlook) how much they
influence what their patients choose to talk about.
In a host of discreet ways, we give clues—a nod, a
move in the chair, a line of questioning pursued or
ignored, a clearing of the throat a rise of the eye-
brows, or, alas, an impassive silence, our particular
"face of stone." And, of course, before the patient
comes to the office, so that he or she may "free
associate" exuberantly—one thought after another,
a jumble of ideas and symbolic metaphors and
memories and fantasies and dreams suddenly re-
called, all coming out in a tumble—there have been
conversations, or those moments of witness we all
have: the news heard or read about; or an incident
observed, however trivial or unrelated, apparently,
to the thrust of one's "problems." We don't carry
on with ourselves extended monologues; nor do we,
even with the doctor, offer a soliloquy, which it is
his or her duty and challenge to "interpret." We are
constantly engaged in *conversations;* we go back
and forth, stop, go blank, so to speak, resume, inter-
rupt one "voice" with another, making quite sure,
for a number of reasons, that a differing or opposing
opinion gets expressed—by us, speaking to ourselves, cautioning or warning ourselves against ourselves.

Williams won't let Gurlie's mind run amok with
its search, its importunate demands; she is, again,

not going to be a polemical caricature, or the means by which a novelist presents his flashy psychological "insights." Similarly, Joe's pensive side is not given free rein — and the temptation must have been substantial, because the risk would be low (it is his nature, well presented) and the likelihood of approval substantial: Williams the known experimenter, the avant-garde poet, the man who had met or knew well Pound and Joyce and Gertrude Stein and on and on, has done a long and faithful job of evoking the "consciousness" of an immigrant American workingman, thereby (in the 1920s and 1930s, when Freud was arriving in America as a conqueror) having it both ways — loyal to his avowed interest in rendering what is uniquely American, but quite able to prove himself a man who knows well, and from a distance belongs to, the boldly empirical and imaginative expatriate, literary world of Paris. Instead we get constant, and sometimes distracting interruptions, shifts of perspective, and occasionally gratuitous, one can argue, interventions of plot movement or authorial observation. When Joe is beginning to lash out at "those bums," his fellow working men, the future members of labor unions, Gurlie all too quickly and unnecessarily, it can be argued, breaks in: "Take it, she said, seeming to read his thoughts. You are better than any of them, you have the brains." Have we,

thereby, been thwarted from a "deeper" awareness of the "roots" of Joe's "attitudes"? Or is her
interference, as presented to the reader, itself an
"in-depth" (as we would clumsily say) interpre-
tive stroke?

The author wants to remind us, perhaps, that Joe
and Gurlie are constantly in touch with each other,
even if he or she appears to be utterly self-pre-
occupied. Nor will the dichotomy of her as the
shrill, pushy one and he as the reluctantly com-
pliant one quite work. He recognizes her driving
nature for what it is, and even becomes conde-
scending (rather than overtly angry with her) in his
thoughts; she is guilty of simplifications, he knows,
and there is little he can do about it. "But he caught
the fire," the author lets us know — and in fact he has
all along been a proud, somewhat isolated man who
keeps his own counsel, so far as his fellow printers
go, and who has very high standards for himself.
His wife's coaxing is, therefore, not unfamiliar to
him; he has been a rather stern judge of himself,
and he can equal Gurlie in what he expects of himself. When she comes up with the political rhetoric
congenial to all "captains of industry," not to mention those who merely aspire to be a sergeant, or
maybe with luck a lieutenant, he is attentive. She
talks about America being a "free country" — in the
sense that each of us is able to push ahead; if one

hesitates, one gets nowhere—and needless to say, the next guy will be in there, fighting hard, and maybe below the belt, for his.

Joe doesn't want the baby to suffer the consequences of any argument he might be tempted to have with his wife. She is willing to make her social and economic comments personal: "You owe it to me to fight." He feels that *they* owe it to their child not to fight with each other. But the author makes clear that Gurlie was not only demanding, but giving; again, she loved Joe, and correctly sensed his ability to launch himself as a businessman. If he was "a working man," then "very deep inside him moved another man"—by which the author does not mean that it was Gurlie who "made" Joe into what he becomes in the course of the trilogy, by taking advantage of qualities in him already there. He responds not only to her, or even to himself, his side that is buried "very deep inside," but to the world of American business, which Williams takes great pain to describe: its self-serving rhetoric; its affinity for political manipulation; its disdain for the weak and its grudging respect for anyone, however much a competitor or ideologically antagonistic, who possesses power. And he responds to his children, those objects of faith a secular world uses at once so sincerely, desperately, disarmingly, and cleverly. His wife has told him nothing about them he doesn't already know: their fate is very much at stake; if, somehow, his fortunes don't improve, the baby nearby and her older sister will have one kind, as opposed to another kind, of life. In a terse sentence, which he lets stand as a whole paragraph, Williams observes: "And the baby slept while about its head a drama that was its future had begun." Whole books on "child development" have said less.

Williams does not spare us such sentences. He has a way of condensing all sorts of issues into a brief incident or into a phrase or two, often spoken by one of his characters, rather than himself as the narrator; that is to say, he is a novelist who has a sharp eye for that intersection of the private and the public which determines the moral character of human beings: how they combine their obligations to the demands of the world with their sense of what they want for themselves and those they call their own. When Joe walks to work, his thoughts carry him to fishing, which he loves; but no, "a man must keep on, he must keep on working and then, finally, he will see the light." Such "stern self-denial," as the author calls it, doesn't easily get confined to a factory. It isn't a very long step from a "work ethic" to a whole manner of child-rearing — though, again, one can go through the "literature" and see precious little acknowledgement by child psychiatrists of how variously and significantly a man's job, and his attitude toward that job, affects the psychological development of his young children.[3] If the man has had troubles with his mother or father, yes; then he is judged as compelled unwittingly to reenact one or another kind of "oedipal drama"; but if he has a particular notion of what his responsibilities are in a factory, *and* if the factory owners allow him only a certain way of discharging those responsibilities (clock in, leave not one minute early, do exactly what so-and-so says, regardless of whether it makes any sense, all so that he may bring home a wage which is utterly inadequate), then that is a "sociological" matter, rather than one for those interested in *infants*.

For Williams the fatalistic surrender of Joe to the demands of work is an important part of the child Flossie's life. After Joe promises himself that one day "the light" will be visible, he becomes more precise with himself: he will "come out of poverty," and then he'll be in a position "to keep everyone happy." And even more to the point, he asks himself: "What is lovelier than a place in the country with small children playing in the grass, or picking flowers — that is, wild flowers and peonies." With the end of *White Mule* his "small children" are in a country place; and with the end of the trilogy, his older children will have spent many seasons at *their* place in the country. But that is the future. Right now Joe is still torn, undecided. Suddenly he shifts his angle of vision drastically. He is still thinking about children, his and everyone else's, but they aren't just having a grand time in a meadow: "That's the trouble, they always want to take things, anything — everything." Let Rousseau and any of his intellectual descendants who happened to be around in the 1890s talk of the innocence of children; Joe is quite convinced that "they have to be taught not to take the things that are planted in the gardens — they are children." He becomes interestingly specific: "They want to take things that don't belong to them."

It turns out that Joe does not take such a tough, "realistic" view of children for no reason at all. His mind has taken him that far because it has other, quite related, issues to settle. From Flossie and Lottie we are asked to leap toward grown-ups — and without so much as a connective phrase or explanatory transition sentence: "That's the unions. Revolutionists. All the same." And to make us more confused about his view of workers, children, and his own obligations: "That's what she is, a little socialist! He smiled to himself. She's right too. Take everything you can get. Let somebody else plant it and tend to it. Just take it." Abruptly Joe's slightly petulant anger stops. He stares out of a window of the elevated train which, early in the morning, is carrying him to work: one more commuter. The tenement houses stretch on, an endless background for the tired, sad faces of those who, like Joe, are up at about six-thirty and if lucky home at about the same time, with Sunday the only chance to see much of the sun, never mind grass and flowers. "Fools!" he thinks as he scans those faces. He bites his teeth in disgust — at himself as well as those who with him crowd the train. Then he is again back to children, perplexed by their demanding, anarchic side, mindful of how much restraint they must learn, lest they get in serious trouble, and finally, insistent to himself (with no prompting from Gurlie needed) that he will indeed "provide." And then, to close the line of thought, he remarks to himself that "the place for a baby" is not the tenement house he and his family call home, but a place "out in the country."

There isn't much more time for such thinking — and complicated social and psychological analysis. The building is soon there, with its watchmen, which Joe Stecher, like many others, lives in, it can be said; he spends most of his wakeful hours here. Joe feels "in the middle" in that building. He has become a foreman, a manager of sorts. The bosses are on his right, the other workers on his left. And hovering over him, in a way, are not only his wife and children but his own conflicted view of what is right and wrong. In *White Mule*, a novelist tries to indicate the almost hopelessly divided and contradictory allegiances of this man and his wife, and show how such allegiances become a source of anguish for those who hold them, and equally, a

decisive inheritance for their children. Flossie becomes the person she is, to an important degree,
because of the ideological struggles her father,
especially, wages — and lives out. No wonder that
Williams keeps the baby at the center of the story,
even as he concentrates on portraying the lives of
Joe and Gurlie; it is the baby's life that is being
fought for, or argued about. And she, when grown,
will no doubt find it as hard as her father to sort out
self-interest from that generous side children quite
naturally have. If they don't know the value of
things, if they are reckless and heedless, they not
only may trip and fall and become bruised, weak-
ened, badly hurt; they also may rush into each
others' arms, offer impulsively whatever they have
to a friend, neighbor, or even slight acquaintance.

Joe worries about the impulsive inclination children may have to pick flowers, gather what may well
be theirs not to gather; but it is not necessarily
greed, avarice, or a lack of a fitting sense of property — what belongs to whom — that may prompt such
"impulsiveness." One can appear to be grabby on
the spur of the moment because one has all of a sudden met someone quite lovely to whom one wants to
offer something — and a something (the flowers and
plants Joe refers to) that seems near at hand and no
one's in particular. To emphasize the darker side
of a child's "impulsivity" (a word Williams certainly is not tempted to use), and moving along the

scale of abstraction from psychology to political
philosophy, to regard socialism as an expression of
rampant, thoughtless greed, and then to justify
it for oneself and one's little daughter, after having
just criticized it with utmost severity as a destruc-
tively revolutionary approach to life, is to show how
precarious a hold on "reality" even a sound, stable,
and hard-working man has — not because he is
tempted by the "madness" psychiatrists talk about,
but because he has to make sense of the social and
economic "madness" we call "life."

The result is the inconsistency and unpredict-
ability of Joe's attitudes, not only toward socialism
or capitalism, or labor unions and management,
but his own wife and children. He senses Gurlie's
insecurity, the desperation of her pleas and threats,
but he cannot acknowledge some of the important
causes — the sad decline of her family's situation in
Norway, and the last-ditch stand that America rep-
resents for her: I will not have daughters but sons
(she dreamed of six of them), and a husband who
will set up an unshakeable dynasty of sorts here in
America, so that never again will my family be de-
fenseless, adrift in a foreign land, and unsure of
what the next day will bring. When she becomes
most demanding, he begs off a bit, but thinks highly
of her — she is a Viking, and so would naturally
want to win out. It is too much for him to look ruth-
lessly at the world he himself is so much immersed

in. Better to think of his wife as a fighter (and that
is that) than a person who strikes out because she
feels frightened and vulnerable. Similarly, Gurlie's
gentleness is at times misunderstood or ignored;
she fights for life, for recognition, for her place in
every possible sun: the family, the neighborhood,
the city or town. Doing so, she is acknowledged and
loved by her equally embattled husband. But let
her be more quiet, even contemplative or (specula-
tively in the future) inclined to be carefree (with
flowers, never mind money) and Joe is at a loss:
what has happened to the Gurlie he thinks he knows
so well?

Writing in the 1920s and 1930s, Williams had an
uncanny eye for issues we today consider our very
own. He was interested in that terrain where interior
life merges with the external "facts of life," not to
be confused with the "social factors" which some
psychiatrists all too readily dismiss as merely "superficial," as opposed to the "deep" forces set in
motion by what happens in the privacy of homes
between mothers or fathers and their children.
Williams went to those homes (as opposed to receiving visitors in his office for fifty-minute stretches)
and knew full well that Paterson's social turbulence
and economic strife (or New York City's in the
1890s and thereafter) were an intimate part of the
most private lives of husbands and wives, parents
and children. He is determined to weave into the

Stecher family, into their innermost ruminative moments, the decisive experiences he knew they were having as individuals living at a certain moment in history and under certain circumstances.

An everyday, unsurprising exchange between Joe and Gurlie shows how New York City's tenement neighborhood, and even more broadly, America's economic condition around the turn of the century, work their way into a particular "marital relationship": "Fifty dollars a week. What's the good of talking to you? But we have to live on that. We have to sleep, eat, dress, travel, amuse ourselves on that—that's all we have." To which Gurlie, without flinching, replies: "I don't care what you do. What do I care? I tell you we've got to move. We've got to. Do you understand *that?* Or else the baby will die. It can't live here, I can't take it out into the street every minute. It has no air, it's dying from these rooms. I'm dying. We're all dying here." Joe laconically observes: "You don't look it." And no doubt her hysteria, of an almost calculated kind, one occasionally concludes, is thereby nicely punctured. But she persists, and he, like a therapist, some of us might think, can only keep reminding her of the "reality" they simply have to face. She won't, though; she wants to change "reality," not accept it. She tells her husband to quit if he can't get more money, move up in the firm. Yes, he could quit—but they would starve to death, he reminds her. And she replies without hesitation: "You make me sick," and follows that with her challenge: "Are you afraid?" Soon, as their argument intensifies even further, she threatens to go to his place of business, make demands for him, and by implication, leave the household in search of a destiny of her own as a worker. Somehow, at all costs, they must escape their present fate.

A woman's desperation becomes a man's constant fear. Joe worries that his wife will indeed show up one day at his place of business. He also worries that his daughter somehow is becoming a foil— overlooked and ignored, resented one moment, the next made the ironic excuse for the most strenuous kind of admonitions and petitions. And when a wife and mother feels that she and her family are dying, the daily emotional consequences don't have to be spelled out, and aren't; they take the form of moods: irritability, crankiness, petulance, and melancholy on the part of adults, children, or both.

In the middle of the book a workers' uprising at Joe's plant takes place. Gurlie reads the news: "Strike! Scenes of disorder! Violence! Typographers being imported from Paterson and as far west as Buffalo. Both sides girding their loins. A General Strike among the printers unless the pressman's demands are acceded to by noon tomorrow." Gurlie's mind is with her husband; she does worry for his safety, but more important to her is his involve-

ment with the company—and his co-workers. He
is loyal to the bosses, determined not to strike himself and not to allow the strikers to close down the
company's operations. She senses in his posture
the beginning of a rise: the strike broken (by police),
the bosses grateful, and on and on. The violence in
the air seizes her; she becomes restless, nearly
agitated. She sits in her apartment unable to do
anything, but imagining what others, notably Joe,
are doing: "The enforced inaction all day, violence
within herself, had Gurlie nutty." And the children
quickly respond to their mother's frustrated, dis-
tracted state of mind: "After a while they seemed
to act just as if she wasn't there, amused themselves
with all sorts of little ordinarily forbidden tricks."
Not only do the children get more, perhaps too
much, leeway; they see her pacing back and
forth, obviously excited. And when their father
comes home they see their mother strangely animated. We are told that "Gurlie sat close to her
husband with one hand on his shoulder."

She is excited by the violence Joe had faced down;
he had with determination pushed his way through
the strikers. But Joe wants to forget what happened
at work. He wants to know about the baby's injured finger—which Gurlie had ignored and by her
self-preoccupation had allowed to get uncovered.
When he expresses his concern for Flossie, the
mother is put off and annoyed. Why worry about a

child's finger when it is quite possible that their social and economic fate was being decided downtown? But the father continues to worry—and then considerably frustrates his wife when he tells her that he is tired and wants to go to bed. She lashes out; she is confined to "this prison" while he goes out and tastes the world, takes it on—and then refuses even to let her enjoy vicariously his experiences. She is described as being "beside herself"—and no doubt in today's language, she craved a kind of "liberation" she didn't know precisely how to spell out, and could only visualize in the form of more money, a home of her own in the country, and elevated position for her family in society, rather than an elevated personal situation in which her natural talents or interests could find expression. And marvelously, as the mother struggles with her willfulness, *her* determination "to be," the baby pursues its destiny. Flossie explores relentlessly, gets into everything, her activity a fascinating backdrop for Gurlie's pent-up, fierce ambitiousness: a child and a mother not quite sure where they are going, but each driven hard by impulses that go unchallenged.

Meanwhile, Joe stakes out the beginning of his rise. He stands by his bosses, while all the while aware of how venal they and others can be. One moment he is an eloquent populist, denouncing corruption and exploitation of various sorts. The

next he turns on "the mob," and thereby sets himself up in his mind as "above" all of "them." And in
case he has any doubts, there is Gurlie's version of
populism, for him an especially helpful way of
looking at things. "Everyone is dishonest," she
shouts, and just about everyone cheats, she goes on
to insist—or would, if given half a chance. So,
people have to take what they can get—and if ideal-
istic sacrifice seems an inviting alternative, then
one is a damn fool: just look around and see! This
fluctuating, unstable, but ultimately self-justifying
kind of social and political analysis, taken up almost
in alternation by husband and wife, is accompanied
by shifts and turns in the growth of their two girls—
who, for instance, explore a room or part of a city
park when their parents dream of doing the same
by moving elsewhere, or argue and fight and try to
figure out what is possible and what is strictly
forbidden when their parents attempt to agree on
what America will allow of them or offer them.

In one chapter (XII) Gurlie regards with contempt her own neighbors—herself, really—when
she asks why the poor "huddle all together" and
tolerate the awful, unsanitary, makeshift housing
they occupy. They sicken her, and she insists that
she has no sympathy "for them"—and by implication, indicates that her rather severe tendency to
self-loathing, however covert, will require constant achievements of her husband to be appeased,

if indeed it is possible for anything he does to rid her of such a feeling. In the following chapter, the older daughter quite calmly but brutally claws her young sister—and the little one is virtually scolded by the mother for making too much noise when she bursts into tears. In the jungle one fights to stay alive, even if the price is loneliness and a continuing if unacknowledged sense of shame: all those others who just won't make it—and whom one dare not care a whit about. No wonder those growing up under such circumstances are not exactly encouraged to become the most retiring and peaceful of children.

And so with the rest of us, wherever we stand on those various "scales" social scientists use. I recall a Catholic father I have spent time with; he lives in a suburb to the south of Boston, and works on an assembly line for the Gillette Razor Blade Company. Once, on a Sunday afternoon, he somewhat plaintively asked me this: "How can I teach my children Christ's philosophy when they argue and fight? I know that when they grow up it's dog eat dog out there in the world." He is no socialist critic of America; he is an intensely patriotic man, a veteran of the Korean War, a member of the Knights of Columbus and the American Legion, who at the same time knows what it's like "to try to keep ahead of your bills, and meanwhile people are pushing at each other, all the time pushing." Joe occasionally becomes "romantic"; he tells himself that "wonderful children" are to be found in the most wretched of urban slums. Gurlie is always there to remind him how awful it is to be poor. She will not be carried along on Joe's wave of senti-mental attachment for the impoverished, brutalized wife of one of his drunken former subordinates: if that woman's children or others like them appear "wonderful," that is at best a consolation of the doomed.

As for Gurlie's children, and Flossie in particu-lar, Williams at one point indirectly intervenes to have his say about their future. Gurlie has taken her young child for a checkup (she is a year old). The doctor is old, crusty, opinionated, uninterested in winning admirers. He hands out medical advice — what the child should eat; but he also adds, a bit gratuitously, some more general remarks about children and how they grow up in America. He does not approach Gurlie quite as Dr. Williams described himself doing with his patients in *Life Along the Passaic River*. That is to say, he is more restrained, and also, more discursive; he takes Gurlie to be more his "equal." But he spares no one his blunt analysis: children are "born to be unhappy," he says; moreover, each generation, out of envy, kills the next one's chances of being happy through what is called "child-rearing." The young remind us that time is running out, so we direct our frustration and resentment at them. The doctor is especially hard on schools; he denounces them as "factories of despair," as prisons where children sit and "stupidities . . . drip into their heads one drop at a time until it stupefies them." Then he adds, significantly, "Makes mules of them."

Critics have emphasized that the doctor provides Williams with an opportunity to sound off,[4] and though I have just indicated my agreement, I want to add a qualification: he also gets a chance to caricature both himself and other secular experts — and very important, he shows how a sharp-eyed, thoroughly honest social critic nevertheless cannot extricate himself completely from the very social order he strongly condems — and so, must himself become, at times and without conscious intent, an accomplice of sorts for one like Gurlie, whose ambitions, as they affect her children, are not exactly what the doctor has in mind to recommend. As he takes after "elderly females who are in the menopause," the teachers who attempt to stifle the imagination of schoolchildren, he begins to treat Gurlie as not only a listener but a potential equal: she will listen to him, take his advice, and thereby (at least to a degree) escape the fate most others must suffer. At the end of the visit, unable to diagnose anything specifically wrong with Flossie, he nevertheless recommends a trip to the country. Thereby she will get refreshed, and become more alive, more responsive to the natural world of farms and in Virginia Woolf's phrase, "rounded hills like birds' wings folded," a contrast indeed with the ghetto world of Manhattan.

He has, with that recommendation, nicely moved himself alongside Gurlie; the two of them have no great use for what they see happening around them, but neither is willing to take the decisive step of calling for (and working for) an end to what they together perceive as dishonest or worse. Let's get on top, Gurlie keeps saying to Joe — not that he always needs her harangues. Escape, get out if you can, the doctor says to Gurlie. That same doctor would not offer such advice to the desperate unemployed of Manhattan, or Paterson, New Jersey. He has taken the measure of Gurlie, who, in fact, approaches him as if he were a Dr. Spock. Of course, there was no such authority on child development in the 1890s; as recently as 1938 we had yet to receive in America the succession of books on "baby care" which now do indeed help out countless mothers. Even today Dr. Spock's book, and others like it, are not commonly to be found among the poor. I have never seen his book, in the course of my work with impoverished black and white families in various parts of the United States. The doctor in *White Mule* seems to know that much of Gurlie's trouble as a mother has to do with a driving intention on her part to change the conditions of her life. She couldn't breast-feed her child. She was as finicky in her selection of food for her child as her child was in accepting what was proffered. She needed, the doctor knew, help in becoming more relaxed, more "natural" with her children. But how could she become so, given her unswerving insistence on rising up, changing the whole structure of her life? I recall the words of an unemployed coal miner's wife: "Here in West Virginia if you want your children to get out and become better off, you have to decide that you're going to train them, train them real firm and hard, and even then it may all be for naught. There's only a few of us who can really improve ourselves."

The doctor never tries to let Gurlie know how she, like those schoolteachers he so roundly, and, it can be claimed, conveniently condemns, is also hurting children—two of them, her very own. In a sense the teachers are for him what the Jews or Irish or Italians are for Joe: scapegoats, a means of ridding oneself of anger, bitterness, and not least, the bothersome sense of guilt that goes with a kind of half-knowledge—that it's not really the other immigrants, or the school-teachers, who have the most to gain by a continuation of the *status quo*. One shirks that realization because one has already decided something for oneself: I intended to stay with this system, and as soon as possible be on the top of it, or I intend to be a part-time social critic,

as I pursue my medical work, but go only so far—
lest I, never mind my patients, never get to spend
any time in the refreshing, sustaining countryside.

In the latter part of *White Mule* the author makes
quite clear his conviction that Gurlie must not,
ironically, be allowed to become the reader's all
too convenient equivalent of the Jews and Irish,
or the schoolteachers. She has been from the start
rather too easy to dislike—a woman who won't be
openly affectionate with her husband, who is cold
(in today's word, "rejecting") toward little Flossie,
and who in the crudest words asserts her wish for
a more comfortable life. Joe does a lot of day-
dreaming in the first part of the book; he is naturally
introspective, if not brooding. We get to know how
his mind works, so that when he becomes, in fact
(to a degree, at least), a manipulative, bigoted entrepreneur, ready to turn on his bosses and his
fellow workers alike, in order to carve out for himself a successful business, we at least are aware of
his difficulties, the anguish he sometimes feels,
and not least, the existence of his conscience—
which he has, nevertheless, repeatedly violated.
No such ambiguities seem to characterize Gurlie
for most of the book; she is strident on page one,
and we confidently expect her to remain so—at least
until her behavior softens, as she has promised her
husband it will, upon their *second* arrival: first in
America itself, then the good life, the nice life of

suburbia, which it is the province of the second and
third volumes of the trilogy to portray. But when
she goes off, following the doctor's advice, to Vermont, she shows herself capable of humor, imagination, intelligent observation, and, very touching, a
genuine responsiveness to the landscape — the clean
air which she notices and loves breathing in, the
power of the Hudson as it cuts its way through the
land, and the mystery of the endlessly traveling
sun: in and out of clouds, here then gone, as the
evening asserts itself. She, too, can meditate, be
stirred by beauty, even turn on herself critically —
and in the first volume, well before her husband
has become a "success." The directness she always
had becomes rather appealing when it is not harnessed to what sociologists refer to as "upward
social mobility."

There is, for instance, a moment in the country
when she talks with her new-found friends. She is
still the cynical and stubborn woman who won't, if
she can help it, live a life of poverty or only mar-
ginal comfort. But she is not unable to examine
America carefully, and come up with a devastating
analysis of its history — and for that matter, of her
own as an immigrant. She will have no truck with
sentiment; she, like everyone who comes here
("we are all the same"), had self-improvement as a
goal — the economic kind. "How can we love this
country?" she asks. She insists that few people

really chose uprootedness voluntarily and in some spirit of adventure. The point was to escape — punishment, persecution, famine, and on and on. "We are from Europe," she says, and she sees little chance that even her children or her children's children will feel different (and how wrong she was!): "That old love of home sticks to the second and third generation." This country is "all for greed" she continues; and then comes her more pointed historical analysis, which actually exceeds in historical sweep anything her sometime populist husband has ever come up with: "This wasn't our land. It belonged to the Indians. It will take a long time to get a love for it like we had on the other side." And further: "If you go to jail and you make money anyhow, who cares?" That, for her, is the ultimate corruption of America — a contrast, she believes, with the rural Norway she knew as a child. She goes on to tell how much she loves the outdoors — that is, when there are no disfiguring slums nearby: "To me a tree and a bush can talk" — a comment worthy of both her pediatrician and, be it noted, a poet.

Her "lovely walk" up in Vermont is an occasion for us to see, at some length, her softer, gentler side. She will not be the first bourgeois woman who grabs what she can, who experiences hate toward much of what she continues to grab, and who, every once in a while, desires to shed herself of all she has obtained—in order to feel, even if briefly, the wonder, the "kind of awe" the author describes going through her as she takes in not possessions but the hills, the mists that settle in between them, and a cloudless night sky. And when, at the end of the book, a baseball game has everyone shouting that it was up to a hitter, "now or never, to bring home the bacon," one has begun to forget Gurlie's uncompromising shrillness toward Joe. Both of them, as she argues up in Vermont, never caused the ugly, competitive, almost demonic industrial world of nineteenth and early twentieth century America. Neither of them, she is responsible for reminding us, came here in search of a New Jerusalem. They were not Pilgrims or Puritans, but people dealt a harsh economic blow, hence in search of bread rather than roses. In *White Mule* they prove themselves hardy, obstinate arrivals. Cost what it may, they intend to survive—and do so on America's terms; they will take on and, so far as their lives are concerned, master the leviathan, never persuading themselves that such an effort is like walking some "royal road to romance." [5]

Part Three

Survival in America

Survival in America

The two succeeding volumes in Williams' trilogy devoted to the Stecher family were published, respectively, in 1940 and 1952. Williams originally thought of calling the second novel *A Taste of Fortune*. He was not convinced, when he was finished, that he had equalled the first volume: "I hoped it would be a good book, but it doesn't come up to *White Mule*." Nor did the critics, respectful and approving, go into the raptures that *White Mule* inspired. Anyway, *White Mule* appeared at the height of the Depression, when there was a strong interest on the part of critics in the political and/or proletarian novel, and a lingering interest in novels dealing with immigrant life. A short two years later a whole new period of American history was about to begin. War had started in Europe; America was beginning to re-arm — and with that development, the Great Depression was, at last, coming to an end. James Agee's *Let Us Now Praise Famous Men*, which was published in 1941, for all its uniqueness and brilliance, was virtually ignored; had it been published three or four years earlier, the reception almost certainly would have been quite otherwise.

Not that Williams ever intended to ride the crest of a heightened interest in politically conscious, sociological fiction. The Stecher trilogy, he makes clear in *"White Mule* Versus Poetry,"* was prompted by his desire to harness prose as well as poetry to his continuing struggle on behalf of a distinctively American idiom, which he wanted to comprehend for himself, impart to others, and celebrate: "The writing of the language is what interests me," he says in the essay, "so in working at *White Mule* my greatest concern was to write with attention to marshalling the words into an order which would be free from 'lies.' " Then he turns his attention, in an ironic shift, to what he had previously done: "I had spoken, as John Cournos might have said, for the idealism of America, for the great themes of American life and aspiration in the past, in my 'In the American Grain,' in the foreword to my libretto to 'The First President,' in the appreciation of Alfred Stieglitz. . . ." He goes on to say that he felt it his duty "to include the whole of that in my style." But he clearly felt other duties pressing upon him, too: "I'm a pediatrician," he goes on to say, "I take care of babies and try to make them grow." He knew, one has to keep insisting, long before some authorities on "child development," that those babies grow in response to the widest range of influences—not only, for instance, a mother's psychological "attitude," as determined by her experiences with her own mother, but the world of which she is a part, which is, right off, a "force" the infant will have to contend with: a rich mother, a poor mother, a sophisticated American-born mother, an immigrant mother, a mother who has all the time in the world for her children, and all the money she needs, or a working mother whose labor is poorly rewarded, whose time and energy are almost completely consumed by her job, and so forth.

True, there is a specifically biographical side to the trilogy. Williams knew in 1937, before *White Mule* was published, that he intended to devote three novels to a family very much like his wife's. Flossie is Mrs. Williams, and her parents are Joe and Gurlie Stecher. But Williams also drew upon a wider circle of friends, acquaintances, neighbors, patients. What he calls the "detail" is his own: "Some of the conversation was put down verbatim from things said to me by my patients." And he cannot, once again, abstain from indicating how much he owes to those patients, how much they have told him, how inspired he found himself by the twists and turns of their lives, the modest but informative drama he heard unfolded by them— and how tired he was made by their demands. It took, as he put it, "long years of heartbreak," for him to learn how to draw upon his medical work when he found time to sit and write. "Bits here and there date back thirty years," he tells us — making it quite clear that he was emphatically not responding to any particular "moment" in American history, but rather, to the larger thrust of that history as it works its way, quietly and often without notice, into the lives of all of us: the values we choose to have, the ways we regard one another, not to mention the kind of work we find (or don't find) available.

When Williams mentioned John Cournos, he no doubt had in mind that novelist's trilogy, which also deals with immigrant life in America: *The Mask* (1919); *The Wall* (1920); and *Babel* (1922). Williams may have been indirectly responding to a critique he had reason to believe Cournos would have been quick to make of "the idealism of America" which *In The American Grain,* for example, does indeed portray. Cournos' three novels strike hard at America and what it does to those who come here out of desperation. There is precious little "idealism" to be found in any part of the trilogy. In fact, the central character, John Gombarov, an emigré from Russia, in many respects views America as Gurlie does: a nation in which greed and competitiveness are rampant; a nation whose "soul" has been lost; a nation to which people come for good reason — but which they never really end up respecting and loving. Cournos stresses the condescension and worse visited upon immigrants by native Americans. He draws in detail a sordid picture of slum life — people brutalized every day by the rapacity of capitalism as it makes its requirements felt in dozens of ways: pitiful wages, unemployment, exorbitant rents for the flimsiest of housing, and so on. Gurlie may have dreamed that it would all turn out different, that America would become a *home,* as well as a place where the streets were lined with plenty of coins, if not gold. But the reality of American life did not escape her, once she had a chance to look things over. And Joe, too, was not mesmerized by lofty American ideals; in fact, his turning away from Gompers can be understood as something more than a self-serving "adjustment" of ideological perspective to the needs of a business career. Gompers had lectured immigrant workers long and hard: they must put aside their old-world habits and customs in order to become American. Joe was becoming American all right, but without any illusion that "the new heaven and new earth" of the Apocrypha was around a nearby corner.

Cournos eventually has his hero flee America; he feels himself becoming as calculating and cruel, as tough-fisted and callous, as everyone else — so, back to Europe. Not that such a return is a "solu-

tion"; still, the trilogy was uncompromising in its
depiction of early twentieth century capitalist
brutishness — and the novelist's willingness to re-
verse things, take his injured but sensitive hero
back to Europe, was no mere indulgence in "es-
capism," but a bold and rather original attempt to
draw the line on the imperative of Americanization, so celebrated, or at the very least, accepted as
a realistic necessity, by various essayists and novelists. Jacob Riis, for instance, in *The Making of An
American,* does not deny much of what Cournos describes, but he cannot conceive of an alternative for
any immigrant; he or she simply must be "made"!
Even Gertrude Stein's *The Making of Americans,* a
long and hard-to-fathom attempt to show how heavily abstractions like "time" and "history" weigh on
family life, shuns any possibility of *choice.* The
Hersland family has come here, and they will stay.
Their ways of thinking will soon enough respond
to the carefully delineated nuances of American
life, as it is offered the reader at great length and in
minute (and endlessly repetitive and sometimes
murky) detail. In fact, her novel is, among other
things, a way of indicating just how boxed in a
family becomes, once it has been transplanted
from a particular environment to another. The point
is to survive, and quick-growing, adaptive seeds
that we are, we take root almost anywhere, or so she
believes; and she spends hundreds of pages drill-

ing into us her version of the sun shining, the water
falling, the earth nourishing those seeds: life as
nothing more than the repetition of certain con-
stants—hence the much discussed "abstract" style
of her writing.[1]

Unlike Stein, whose writing intrigued him,[2] Williams was a more traditional story-teller, interested
in the particularity of his chosen characters. And
unlike Cournos, he was not prepared to devote himself to an unsparing, unqualified assault on just
about every aspect of American life—with the final
judgment of exile as a summation. But he did de-
liver the manuscript of *White Mule* to his publisher,
James Laughlin, in 1937, however long the gesta-
tion of the story, and however various, personal, and
idiosyncratic the sources of inspiration; so he could
not help responding to what was happening at that
time in Paterson—the strikes, the severe economic
recession, the bread-lines, and very important, the
sense of futility and hopelessness which the children
he treated unquestionably picked up and made their
own—our so-called "Depression babies." I have,
in recent years, heard many factory workers refer
to themselves that way—enough of them that I am
surprised when I don't hear one use the term. "You
want to know about my childhood, and my husband's," a woman asked me about the time I was
reading and re-reading Dr. Williams' trilogy; then
she went on only long enough to make her emphatic

summary: "Well I'll tell you; we were Depression babies, and you don't forget that for the rest of your life." That mother is Polish, not like Gurlie of Norwegian stock, but she can't shake off the cynicism she feels about this country any more than Gurlie could. Williams was saying in his trilogy that no one can—no one can ignore or forget the social and economic circumstances they face and once faced and always will face. Even triumph, he points out in *The Build-Up*, is an obsessive, almost maniacal denial of defeat—rather than a refuge or sanctuary finally obtained. Unquestionably Williams is more critical of America in this trilogy than he'd ever before been, even if he doesn't quite meet Cournos more than halfway, or John Dos Passos, either— and he also wrote a trilogy in the 1930s which deserves comparison with the one Williams gave over to the Stecher family and its involvement with American life.

The three-volume *U.S.A.* was published in 1937, just before *White Mule*. The first volume, *The 42nd Parallel*, had appeared in 1930; *Nineteen Nineteen* followed in 1932, and *The Big Money* in 1936. Dos Passos was of course far more political than Williams; his trilogy, like *Manhattan Transfer* before it, is outspokenly Marxist-Anarchist in its position vis-à-vis American capitalism. But he was, like Williams, akin in ways to Walt Whitman; what Dos Passos could not see in America, because of its

corrupting industrial order, he was quite prepared
to see in Russia and wax lyrical about: "the mag-
nificent energies of the Russian people." And to
what were those energies bent, now that (in 1928)
the revolution seemed secure — unthreatened, that
is, by the capitalist West? "Making life worth living" was the answer. The America he presents in
U.S.A. has betrayed Whitman's hopes — the hopes
of a succession of prophets who hailed the people,
and hailed America as a nation "of, by, and for the
people." It is the melancholy task of the realistic
and socially-conscious writer, Dos Passos indicates
in his trilogy, to remind his readers with all the
skill he can muster what their country, what they
as citizens of it, are coming to.

In a sense, then, U.S.A. is also about "the making
of Americans," a trilogy about a nation's seemingly
irreversible decline and fall. And a far more aspiring and fervent trilogy; Dos Passos intended a
massive indictment of the nation whose initials he
gave to the entire scope of his narrative. Williams
wants us to know that the Stechers were beginning
to "make it" at a certain stage of their lives: they
were "in the money." There is no great compli-
ment intended thereby; Williams was not a starry-
eyed apologist for American materialism. But if the
Stechers are no Horatio Algers, or Andrew Carne-
gies, they are not shown to be decadent, mean, or
vicious, either. As a matter of fact, for all the things

they do to get where they are, they resist even such
epithets as "hypocrite"; they don't even pretend to
righteousness. Williams offers in them Americans
who have no intention of hiding from themselves
the nature of the assertive self-enhancement they
practice in order to get "in the money" and manage
a "build-up."

Dos Passos is polemical; his "big money" is
tainted money, obtained through the sweat of others,
who are left virtually penniless. J. Ward Moorehouse, Dos Passos' businessman in *The 42nd Parallel* who rises from poverty to wealth and power, is
no immigrant, like Joe Stecher; he is also not in
the least appealing. Nor is his wife Annabelle at
all interesting, never mind attractive. Dos Passos
wanted his readers to remember how wicked and
devious his characters are, reflecting the world
they have come so to dominate. Even when they
were young and first acquainted, the Moorehouses
never really were honest with each other; they
tricked and deceived their way into a marriage,
then a life. Dos Passos is extraordinarily compelling
as a satirist; he can weave the banalities and clichés
of a given culture into the empty, sordid lives of
those who think they are original, or setting the pace
for others, but who in fact are servile instruments of
a given social order. Moorehouse talks to himself
about "The Strenuous Life," which he, like President Theodore Roosevelt, will live. He is given to

self-deluding, sticky sentimentality, not unlike the
kind one hears on soap-operas. Maybe he should
be a songwriter, the young Moorehouse thought;
and as a youth he claimed he wanted to meet and
marry a simple, good, pure girl—a "lovely girl"
with whom he could live happily ever after. All
the while, of course, he had begun contriving,
scheming, pushing aside anyone in sight, and moving his way up. He never was "innocent," never
honest with himself, his wife, or the people he as
a businessman dealt with. Eventually he became
a Public Relations Counsel, for his creator the ultimate in the slick, the phony, the misleading and
the conscienceless.

It is not that Dos Passos hasn't the capacity as a
novelist to get close to such a character, understand him objectively if not sympathetically. All
lives are complicated; the source of Moorehouse's
illusions, as with anyone else's, cannot be attributed
to facile psychological or sociological "explanations." He, too, is entitled to the novelist's capacity
for complexity, his taste for ambiguity. But Dos
Passos insists that some of us, early on, become for
all practical purposes wholly identified with "the
machine," the demanding, covetous industrialism
which shapes the imagery not only of paid apolo-
gists but children and those who educate them:
parents who know that one either "adjusts," or goes
hungry, and schoolteachers who know they must

watch out when they talk about what our society is like, what it has a right to ask of us — lest they quite soon be out of work themselves. Moorehouse, we come to realize, was an intelligent man of quick reflexes who had a sharp eye for his own best interests. But his more spectacularly successful accommodation to the "system" is not meant to be a caricature, hence an acid portrait, in the tradition, say, of George Grosz, from which the rest of us can take comfort in dissociating ourselves. Dos Passos is a good enough novelist to make most of us squirm a bit, even today, when we read of such a man's social and economic rise.

The 42nd Parallel also offers us Fenian McCreary, whose uncle, like the Joe Stecher of *In the Money,* owns a printing shop. But the uncle is an avowed socialist, and Mac, as Fenian McCreary is called, becomes one, too. He is a wobblie, a member of the I.W.W. He will fight capitalism, rather than discover in the interstices of the system a fine, profitable place for himself. And he does — for a while. Soon, however, he has made a girl pregnant, so they marry, and in no time she is complaining about his low wages and his socialist inclinations. Why doesn't he face up to his "responsibilities"; and anyway, what about the child, will the I.W.W. feed and clothe the baby? Mac eventually realizes that he has "sold out"; even without his wife's nagging, he has gradually withdrawn from the more explicit and risky kind of social protest. He ends up leaving her, and for a while one believes that he will, as he says, "work for the movement." He goes to Mexico, hoping to link arms with Zapata and his cohorts. But he is an Anglo, and rather quickly it becomes clear that he can go far in Mexico City. Never a Moorehouse, he nevertheless flees Mexico City when a revolution threatens, and is all too willing to contemplate returning when a counter-revolution takes place. Why should he return to the United States when he is doing so well in Mexico — when he is, in fact, a capitalist himself by now, a man with too much to lose? Best to stay in Mexico and prosper.

The contrast with the Stechers is significant. Dos Passos' trilogy is almost always included in lists of "political novels" or "radical novels"; Williams' trilogy, practically never.[3] Yet, Williams was strongly critical of the American economic system in the 1930s; if he never went as far as his friend Ezra Pound, he did, as noted earlier, indeed rail against usury in *Paterson,* and, along with his good and devoted friend and publisher James Laughlin, he advocated a serious kind of reform — the gist of which was that the productive capacity of the nation be geared toward supplying people with what they needed to live decently, rather than to the fluctuations in the stock market or the decisions of executives who think of profits first, last, and always. I do

think, however, that he was less able than Dos
Passos and others to give himself over to political
or economic abstractions, however worthy and
illuminating. Dos Passos, at least for a while, saw
each of us swallowed up by the capitalist behe-
moth; he wanted in his novels to show just how that
outcome came about. Williams as a doctor was intimately connected to the lives of all sorts of "vic-
tims"; he could not achieve the distance—in real
life or in his writing—that Dos Passos manages.
The more time he spends with his characters (and
a trilogy compels a long time), the less disposed he
is to become unremittingly scornful or satirical
toward anyone.

Gurlie at first surprises, even shocks us. Williams
seems intent on doing something even more "radical" than Dos Passos ever attempted; we will be
shown how economic materialism infects and kills
a mother's relationship with her infant child. "Is
nothing sacred?" the populist Tom Watson screamed
in the first phase of his career. No, nothing is, he
later concluded—and proceeded to "sell out," like
one of Dos Passos' figures.[4] But even Mr. Moorehouse clings to certain pieties and does his apparent
best to live up to their demands: the virtues associated with home, mother, apple pie. And Dos
Passos never really calls him or anyone else to
count for the way they actually end up doing so,
spending their days and nights as husbands and

fathers. When Mac goes to Mexico he, of course, leaves behind a wife and child. What happens to that child? How does the mother get along with her? One can picture a mother complaining to her husband about his idealism—and not only caring deeply for those children, but of all ironies, instilling a certain limited, cautious idealism in them. Dos Passos is chiefly interested in Mac's social and economic career; Williams might have delighted in constructing a novel around the life of Mac's child, and, perhaps, the wife he left. Perhaps such a novel would have been even more tellingly "radical"— but would not meet the criteria some have for what constitutes a "radical novel."

When a novelist permits himself to become forcefully ideological, no matter in how valuable a cause, he makes a substantial professional sacrifice. He denies himself the chance to look at certain corners of his characters' lives; even a trilogy can allow just so many sub-plots, so much analytic scrutiny of this or that individual's mental or social life. When Williams started out with Flossie's birth, and in his mind kept her developing childhood as a sort of harness for himself—he could only stray so far from her—he forsook in the trilogy sustained political and economic criticism for psychological and social ambiguity. He makes it clear in the essay he wrote, *"White Mule* Versus Poetry," that he was not at all, from the start, going to *devote* himself to

the baby; by the end of the third novel "the baby
as a principal character" will be gone—not, incidentally, replaced by an older child or youth. For
him an infant's birth, and later, her emergence as a
specific (demanding, complaining, loving) child is
an occasion for others to assert themselves, reveal
themselves, and more introspectively, find out
about themselves. Williams might have written a
whole novel (I doubt a trilogy) in the vein of the
first chapter of *White Mule*, "To Be." But he chose
not to do so. He does from time to time in the three
novels come directly back to Flossie, put himself
and hopefully his readers in her mind as she begins
to comprehend the world, as she literally and symbolically stands up on her own feet—first the body,
then the mind, as it starts leaving the familiar if
not always comfortable terrain of a particular family
for "life" as others live it elsewhere. But he wants
to roam more freely than a strictly psychological
novel would allow. (With respect to ideological
thinking, politics is but one of several focuses; psychology, these days, is another.) It was a desire and
inclination which may have cost him, as a novelist,
the attribution of "great." One thinks of Joyce's or
Proust's single-minded dedication to a particular
viewpoint—accompanied, naturally, by genuine
vision and the craftsman's skill. For all his interest
in American regionalism, however, Williams as a
novelist had Henry James' passion: "the manners,

the manners" obsessed the Anglophiliac exile from America, and with respect to far different turf, *Paterson* and the Stecher trilogy show a similar preoccupation.

Neither *In The Money* nor *The Build-Up* strikes any new theme; presumably a trilogy enables a writer to work with themes he has judged one novel incapable of developing adequately. Gurlie never quite gets over her dilemma: how to justify one's ambitions, especially when they get fulfilled, as they do by the end of the trilogy. She never speaks like Andreas Veland, a fellow Norwegian immigrant who, in *Recollections of an Immigrant* (1929), constantly chided those who tended to harbor a romantic attachment to the "old country." Like Gompers (especially in his *Seventy Years of Life and Labor*) Veland advocated complete accommodation to America's "standards of work." One would think that a labor organizer, as Gompers for a time was, might have remembered even in his old age how unjust, to say the least, those "standards" were—the ideological content, however indirect, of a nation's political and economic life. When there is a split in such content, when we hear that "all men are created equal," but that the rich and powerful can show utter contempt for their fellow citizens and by and large get away with it, then the grounds for mixed or contradictory feelings have been established.

Gurlie would laugh at Gompers and Veland; she would claim that she was, like them, anxious to become utterly, completely American—that is, she would have her husband beg, borrow, and virtually steal, if need be, in order to secure for his family the money, the "build-up" we find him eventually coming forth with. But she is herself, and not simply the foil of a Dr. Williams who had contempt for what he saw happening to America in the 1930s. Why shouldn't she claw her way up, scramble furiously and unrelentingly, until she is a respected member of an ever so well bred world, the members of which can, of course, proceed to look down upon those below them, who are "coarse" or "bold," or too "aggressive" or blatantly "money-conscious" —and at the same time, being the particular person she was, have the utmost contempt for a nation which gives such sanction to her and her ilk? Gurlie embraces what she also disdains—and maybe Dr. Williams was candidly self-critical enough to know that he, like the rest of us, is caught up, one way or another, in that same dilemma.

In order to justify her ambitions Gurlie falls back on the children—they need this or that—and on her husband, who is, she insists, deserving of a much better life than the one he has. What they need, what she needs, she also rather persistently insists, is not merely a bigger house, filled with nice furniture, but a redemptive experience—a summer retreat which is something much more than a second home. Her preoccupation with the virtues of rural life is fascinating; at the very beginning—on the occasion of her first trip to the country—she is shrewdly discerning: life can be hard under the exceedingly primitive circumstances one finds. But as Joe begins to accomplish his deals and get some-where, she forgets those disadvantages—not out of calculation, either. She genuinely likes village life in Vermont; it is as if her normally critical eye is suddenly closed tight. The nostalgic love for Nor-way finds expression in the hills of New England—and further, a woman apparently driven by demons can, for a change, relax: no invidious comparisons with the country people whom she opens up to, and with whose children her daughters play; and no sense of desperation or worthlessness as she goes through the day. She is content. The world around her seems lovely, inviting, reassuring. At last her self-doubt seems banished; she is a person of means, and she knows it because others know it. No matter how poor she may feel, in comparison to wealthy or well-to-do urban or suburban families, when she comes to the country she is the rich visitor, possessed of a degree of sophistication which causes awe in her humble country hosts or neighbors. Perhaps there are a few implications in her experience, her "adjustment," for psychiatrists: the social basis of psychological moods.

Why does this smart woman fail to find malice,
deceit and worse up in Vermont or in the rural
country beyond New York City? Was Winesburg,
Ohio, a very special place? Does the Gothic rural
South of Flannery O'Connor or Carson McCullers
not, in fact, exist? Did another immigrant, Constan-
tine Panunzio, err blatantly, in his book, *The Soul
of an Immigrant,* when he wrote:

It is a prevalent idea that the city is the abode of wicked-
ness and vice, while the country life is free from temptations of this sort. This may be true in some communities
in which I have not been privileged to live, but it is
certainly not so of Staceyville. I have never in all my life
heard such obscene, filthy, profane language as I heard
used by men of that village. . . . The women smoke
odoriferous old pipes. Liquor flowed freely, though it
was prohibited in Maine. . . . From these people I
learned my first lessons in American life and manners.

Raymond Williams' *The Country and the City* is
chiefly concerned with the English experience,
though the author, possessed of a broad historical
sensibility, draws upon Greek and Roman myths,
and, further, connects the writing of English poets
and novelists to the concrete political and economic
circumstances which prevailed on mainland Europe
as well as the British Isles.[5] There is no reason to
make an exception of this country; Raymond Williams' analysis applies quite well to William Carlos
Williams' trilogy, except that the novelist, it can be

claimed, knew quite consciously what he was doing.
That is, he did not himself believe and advocate
what he has Gurlie espouse. We know from *Paterson* and *Life Along the Passaic River* that he was not
that tempted either by Whitman's version of man's
nature or of America. He refuses the temptation
to separate man from society, to disentangle "evil"
from "good." [6] The Passaic river, which Williams
could certainly portray on canvas as an almost idyllic
stream running through Eden, was the same river
to which men brought—themselves, in all the willfulness and worse he knew them, *us*, to possess, no
matter who rules, and in what (ideological) name.
His stories are not only about industrialization, the
progressive defilement of rustic beauty and innocence. Some of his characters defy their surroundings: the discontent of, say, Gurlie, never quite dis-
appears—even when she is quite well off, and even
when she is in the country. "The Stechers were no
more than city folks," we are told toward the end of
The Build-Up. And even though they go to the
country often, they don't "know much" about it.
They love the peace and serenity they find, but do
not confuse themselves with (and are not confused
by the author with) "the natives," as he refers to
them in *The Build-Up*, who don't "think much" of
the beauty around them, but rather, go on to live
their lives, which are not any less complicated or
troubled than those of the men and women who

come by on weekends or in the summer for "rest."

The tone Williams achieves in *The Build-Up*, which has a good number of rural scenes, tells a lot about what he did believe about the effect of a particular environment on the thoughts and actions of individuals. None of the characters completely changes; only to a degree are there modifications of attitude or action. Joe continues to make more and more money. Gurlie learns with each year how to live with that money, how to say goodbye to old appetites, satisfy new appetites, and keep an eye out for yet additional possibilities. For all her delight in the social position she has, Gurlie continues to look back at Norway with yearning; and she never ceases her indirect assaults on the very society she wants so much to become part of—the top part of. "All those things a European must lose to become an American, an American!" Gurlie exclaims — at a time when at last she lives quite comfortably in the suburbs as the wife of a man who is not simply making money, but is a well-established businessman who has demonstrated for a number of years that he can and will continue to keep his family in solid comfort. If Williams is not too strongly disposed to Gurlie, then perhaps (it can be argued) her virtual contempt for this country, and her dream that one day she might return triumphant to Norway, with her American dollars to perch herself high up socially, may be responsible for a certain prejudice on the part of a man who wrote *In the American Grain,* and who took after any number of American-born writers, friend or foe, who chose to cross the Atlantic and live in London, Paris, Rome.

But I doubt such was Williams' bias. Gurlie's capacity simultaneously to dislike what she strives hard to become part of makes her, in her creator's mind, simply another interesting human being. And he makes clear that the issue is not his own ideological defense of America, but his responsibility as a novelist interested in convincing character portrayal. Gurlie is proud, he keeps reminding us—is and was and will continue to be. So with Joe; he is less outspoken about what he likes or doesn't like, but it is his pride which, ultimately, prompts and sustains him in the fiercely competitive business world—as the author patiently but without didactic insistence shows in the second volume of his trilogy. Especially noteworthy in that regard, for us who have had to suffer the Nixon presidency, is the scene with Theodore Roosevelt in the Oval Room of the White House. Joe has known about the illegal and collusive practices which have enabled his bosses to obtain government contracts. He has decided to set up his own business, aided by a backer, and to bid for those contracts against his former employers. They, in turn, decide to exert influence in Washington, and

the language they use to justify their crooked course
of action is revealing. Williams again indicates his
conviction that even liars or thieves have to speak
to themselves and one another, have to come up
with words that give sanction to deeds. And those
words are believed, no matter how absurd or ludi-
crous or saturated with rationalizations or worse.

I spent years in the South talking to Klansmen,
among others. They were masters at pietistic rhetoric; and outsiders are wrong if they think the
slogans and night-time, ritualistic orations were
mere window-dressing, elaborate pretenses in-
dulged in by craven men, intent on defending their
social or economic position. There was plenty of
that—plenty of defense, plenty of effort to stay a
rung or two higher than "them" on various ladders.
But there was also a deeply felt conviction: this I
really do believe and want to uphold. Likewise
with the Rotarians and Optimists whom I met
among the White Citizens Councils in Mississippi
during the early 1960s. Their words, with reference
to blacks, were not unlike the ones Dr. Williams has
his conspiring businessmen use when they talk
about their plan to stifle competition, wipe out the
aspiring Joe Stecher, and secure for themselves,
once again, what Harry Truman used to call a
"vested interest." "We can't allow such disloyalty
to succeed," one man says to another—and then the
ultimate condemnation: "It's immoral." What fol-

lows is neutral language which enables the crook
to prove that he and his kind are not immoral: "No
matter what slight irregularities of procedure he
[Stecher] may uncover, whatever we have done that
the government disapproves of can be explained on
a basis of different standards. . . ." It all comes
down, he adds, to "a different way of looking at the
same things."

The author had lived through Teapot Dome, but
had no reason to know how accurately he would
forecast the cool, slippery language of our time:
"standards," "procedure," "slight irregularity," all
used in the interest of a larger, moral vision—and
so that loyalty to the vision would prevail. ("A
generation of peace with prosperity," we were told
again and again.) Nor did Williams have any right
to know how interesting to us, in the 1970s, his
description of Joe Stecher's meeting with the President of the United States, Mr. Theodore Roosevelt,
would turn out to be. The novelist's restraint is all-
important. He resists the temptation to caricature,
satire, parody. Joe is quiet, respectful, obliging. He
is not awed by the President, but he is not the agent
of a sarcastic or cynical writer, out to show how
phony and hypocritical American political life is.
Not that Williams doesn't recognize just that, the
fraud that characterizes the high and mighty (both
men and institutions). In *Life Along the Passaic
River* he tried to avoid sentiment in his presentation

of the working class. With the President of the
United States he is equally canny; one finds the
first Roosevelt a matter-of-fact, down-to-business
person, questioning Stecher briefly and shrewdly.
We are not allowed the illusion, pardonable perhaps in a novel, and especially one with a degree
of social consciousness built into it, that the President was preoccupied with Joe Stecher and his
problems. The President is a king constantly peti-
tioned. Anyone who gets into that Oval Office is
but one of a line — a dozen today, a dozen tomorrow,
and so on with a given President for from four to
eight years.

"It is my policy," the President says at one point,
and Joe can only nod and hope that he will be the
beneficiary. At the end he decides he doesn't like
Roosevelt: "Too much noise, big ideas." But his
reasons for disliking the man and his policies are
not abstract or explicitly political. Joe's pride in
himself, his unwillingness to bow before anyone,
his suspicion of all who put on airs or assert too
officiously *their* pride, combine to make him ill at
ease as he hears this potentate coming down on his
side of the fence. Joe wants to be known as a man
who takes painstaking care that every detail of his
work is correct, even exemplary. He can persuade
himself that he ought to make as much money as he
can, but he cannot get rid of one of the "needs"
Simone Weil specifies as utterly essential to a per-

son's dignity—his or her desire for excellence,
for doing something well, however small and
apparently insignificant. The peasants and factory
workers Mlle. Weil lived with and worked alongside struggled hard to prove to themselves, never
mind show to others, that they could live up to the
demands of their own consciences, even if the re-
ward was not high for doing so. The most humiliat-
ing experience, she observes, for anyone, is to gain
the conviction that what is done matters not at all,
makes no difference in the social order's scheme of
things.[7] John Dos Passos portrayed in some of his
characters such a loss of dignity.

Joe has a craftsman's pride; he has those psychological qualities Mlle. Weil both admires and
knows to be (in this century) in serious jeopardy. It
is that kind of pride, that insistence on self-respect,
that Joe defends at all costs—before the President,
before his wife Gurlie, and not least, in the conversations he holds with himself. His criticism of the
President is not the kind Dos Passos or Sinclair
Lewis would have been tempted to have him make
in novels of theirs. When Roosevelt talks about his
"policy," Joe ignores the self-importance, the
megalomania, the pompous rhetoric which so many,
maybe to a degree all, Presidents display. Rather,
he moves from a President's pronouncement about
a "policy," rendered from on high, to his own concrete appreciation of what is at stake not only for the

President, but himself: "You stop paying attention
to the truth of the detail. You don't look to see
whether that man is an honest man, whether he's
doing the job well or ill. All you care about is My
Policy."

Not unlike many of the working people Mlle.
Weil observed, Joe Stecher sees rather clearly the
implication for ordinary individuals of what plan-
ners of various kinds have in mind, then set in motion. He knows that "the truth of the detail" he
thinks about as he contemplates an earlier version
of the imperial American presidency—in that regard, one of its founding fathers—has to do with
both large and small matters. Everything is grist for
the mill of "policy." In his words: "You plow
straight ahead, flowers, birds' nests, men, lives, op-
portunities—oh well." The last two words convey
his bitter sense of resignation: *he* will never inaugu-
rate a "policy," nor will he fight those who do, at
least not as a social or political activist does. He is
quite cynical about everything from the nature of
Presidential "policy" (and too, the interviews held
in the Oval Office) to the possibility of political reform. Perhaps his cynicism (connected in turn with
a sense of hopelessness about the prospect of any
significant change in the society) enables him to become yet another American entrepreneur. If so,
Williams has done an especially sensitive job of indicating the psychological maneuvers that precede

entry to the bourgeoisie. In fact, that is what his second volume is all about. There are marvelous reveries, which reveal a man's moral conflict, his personal anguish, as he wonders what on earth he ought to do: take on a society he has no great use for, and most likely fail to get very far; throw all principles aside and get, get, get; fight with his wife — an easier adversary than America's economic system; or try to walk gingerly, to straddle, to juggle as best he can, and somehow muddle through — and rise up.

I suppose it can be claimed that there is a parallel between the toddler Flossie of *In the Money* and her father as he comes to terms with his career in the same novel. Both are learning how to achieve whatever independence they can manage. Williams is extraordinarily knowing and convincing when he describes how a young child learns things — walking, talking, and in general, self-care as well as self-assertion. But he knows just as well how workers struggle to do the same: find a place, however small, in some neighborhood's sun. There is a touching moment when the baby lies in bed, alone and supposedly asleep, but watchful and determined not to be ignored. Suddenly she begins to cry, and won't stop. But why? We are told that "she wanted to hear herself again — to know that she was there." We are told that "her own voice killed" that mixture of fear and loneliness a child

can feel when sent to a nap. But this novelist knows
that children don't cry in a psychological vacuum,
so to speak. As she cries her mother also cries —
shouts and screams, as plaintive in her own way, as
frightened and lonely, as her child. And then there
is a father who on the one hand detests rich Fifth
Avenue doctors ("Be sure you'll pay a lot of money
for it so you'll know you're in the hands of a crook")
but also shows up at his backer's club, and never
once, really, holds back in the world of business;
rather, he makes his moves, collects his increasing
amounts of money, and when nervous or ethically
troubled lashes out, *cries* out, at so-called lazy
people — union organizers, with their endless promises, and the whole American scene, which gives
one like him no alternative, or so he believes.

Chapter seventeen of this second novel is especially illuminating; its title is "Night," and it
lends itself perhaps too easily to the various "interpretations" psychiatrists are expected to come up
with. For Williams it is an occasion for suggestive
irony, however, rather than the self-conscious "en-
lightenment" that goes with the explicit theoretical
formulations of social science. As the baby cries,
her parents wonder, as all parents do: what is wrong
and what to do. The father is gentle, the mother
angry. The father wants to soothe, the mother to
teach a lesson, once and for all. The father is in-
tuitive, the mother, it seems, not so. He connects a

child's episode of night-terror with the day's activities. "What frightened her today?" he asks, not out of psychoanalytic "awareness," but out of a parent's natural concern. I recall the words of a sharecropper mother I knew in Mississippi to whom the name Freud meant absolutely nothing: "My baby gets upset, and I know it might be something I've said, or something I've done. I don't think a baby is dumb; a baby will listen, and even if he don't know what the words he's hearing mean, he knows whether there's trouble or whether there isn't any."

As Joe persists, asking about the "trouble" his daughter may have experienced, his wife fights back; and the night, which Williams evokes beautifully—the poet in him wondrously at work—does a bit of fighting, too. "Blackness," he comments at one point, "the mother of sleep, the worst misfortune of all." And so a child can indeed see the dark. Or again: "The insane night prodding the infant with its numb hands. . . ." But Gurlie sees no madness in the night as such; it is her child who has, she suspects, "gone crazy." And why? "It's been too much," she explains. Then she adds: "I wish you would get your business settled so this family can be normal again." Joe's reply is just as instructive: "I wish I'd never seen the Goddamned contract." And more ominously: "I'll move out to Cincinnati or St. Louis or anywhere away from New York. What did you give her to eat for supper?"

Gurlie's comment is, perhaps, familiar to millions of American housewives whose husbands' earnings provide for middle-class living, at however high a personal cost to them as men who are bored with or actively dislike their work. Joe's remarks are more pointed and psychologically suggestive. He realizes that what he is going through has a large but hard-to-specify effect on what his young daughter is then and there going through, in the middle of the night. They are anxiously waiting, he and Gurlie, for their destiny to become, so to speak, manifest. They are, it can be said, in the dark — as frightened and lonely in their respective ways as the narrator tells us Flossie is, in case we don't know it. Even Gurlie's reply to her husband's obviously appropriate question about food gets an answer that indicates how wrought up Gurlie is, at all times, about her position in society: "What do you think I gave her? Caviar?" And Joe is no Caspar Milquetoast at this point: "No, I thought you gave her pork tenderloin and horseradish and sauerkraut," he answers. A little later on, the baby suddenly stops crying and falls dead asleep. Her parents do likewise. Joe has a dream, which the novelist lets stand — no interpretations:

Joe dreamed that he had some sort of a frog-like beast in his hand, only it wasn't a frog, it had a tail and he was holding its head under water, in a pail. "Don't do that," someone said, "that's cruel. You're drowning it." "That's

what I'm trying to do," said Joe. He didn't know why, he
didn't want to drown it but he had to. What else could he
do with it? It wasn't good for anything. Then the thing,
which had a big lizard's mouth, pulled its head to one
side out of the water and looked up at him. That was the
last he remembered—for he woke suddenly.

He was awakened by Gurlie, who in turn had
been awakened by the child, who had in large quan-
tities relieved herself. Joe is glad; now he thinks he
knows why Flossie has been so upset. But Gurlie,
in her own way, has sensed what Joe earlier insisted
upon—the terror in the child. Now that she can relax a bit, feel less accused as a mother, she comes up
with her own version of a psychological observation: "It was the devil in her." But the devil is in
the mother, too. Gurlie dares not say it to her husband, but she is angry with the child. and not only
because there has just been a hard-to-fathom incident. Gurlie wants to live a better life; she feels
tied down by her children, unhappy with her situation, frustrated by the amount of time it is taking
her husband to work his way up, always up. Maybe
she had just gone through a particularly difficult
confrontation with her child, and, too, her husband;
maybe she doesn't always speak to herself with
such a mixture of petulance, anger, and unqualified
self-centeredness. But rather clearly her apparently
transient mood is related to her life as a whole, and
is not therefore something that will simply yield to

the morning's light. Joe's dream, in contrast, was already half forgotten when he awoke; and one can guess that the next day he remembered nothing of the frog. I would assume that the "devil" Gurlie assumed present, was the frog-lizard Joe witnessed in his mind while asleep. And evoked, of course; he used the imagery, as we all do, to speak to himself and say what his mind was trying to come to terms with: himself the frog, anxious to leap, to get out of New York's slums and into the suburbs, and ultimately the country—to jump and jump and jump, in hopes of arriving someplace "better"; and himself the lizard with the big mouth, the lizard who is hungry, greedy, acquisitive—and yes, the lizard who has to be a touch sneaky, a touch smooth, slippery, evasive, agile. On and on go the descriptive words, the associative connections which link a man's sleeping, mental "pictures" to the dilemmas, if not outright conflicts, he is contending with every day. Why, then, would "someone" call him cruel for drowning the lizard-like frog? Joe knows that he didn't want to hurt one of nature's creatures; he "had to." Anyway, the creature wasn't really of any use to anybody. But somehow he fails to submerge and kill the animal; indeed, the animal gets the better of him, and for a second confronts him, thereby ending his dream.

I have some nerve analyzing a dream which Dr. Williams feels no need to explain. I'm not quite

sure why Joe would want to drown an animal if
there wasn't something about it that he found, at
least, distasteful. But why the test of pragmatism:
the question of "what else" he might do with the
creature if he managed to prevail against the force
within him that insisted upon attempting to drown
it? Perhaps Joe is telling himself, is saying loud
and clear, even if indirectly or symbolically, that
when he first began leaping in the business world
he had been as innocent as a dove (or frog). After a
while, though, he became—well, not so innocent,
all of which close scrutiny compels him to acknowledge. And what else can he do—with himself, with his situation as the husband of a particular wife and the father of two young daughters?
Part of him might say: be different, get away from
all this you have become so taken up with. Drown
that part of you and your life. But though he may
want to do so, he also doesn't at all want to do so—
and the presentation to himself of the alternative
at least allows a substantial conflict of his mind,
just stirred up quite significantly, to be acknowledged.

It is hard to put aside one's innocence, one's
open, casual, or honest and uncontrived ways. Yet,
Joe had learned, had decided without deciding,
that he must do just that. He was soon to be well
"in the money"; for him to try to be the same person he once was—energetic, dedicated, not unam-

bitious, but not consumed by ambition either, was
to risk more nights like the one he had just gone
through: a wife's increasingly violent hysteria, a
young daughter's responsive terror, the likelihood
that another daughter would also begin to show
signs of apprehension and worse. His dream tells
him that he isn't the person he once thought he
was. The frog, on close inspection, was something
more than a frog. And as he said to the "someone"
he spoke with — his earlier self, perhaps — it was
now too late for those old moral pieties to work:
do unto others, and so on. We may indeed be cruel
to people as we fight it out with the world, but
what else is there to do, what else can one do,
what else are we "good for"? That is the kind of
question he was learning to ask himself — and
answer with, at the very least, a resigned shrug.
In the late nineteenth and early twentieth centuries
there were serious, passionate anarchists, socialists,
populists who did indeed have important answers
to such a question. But Joe was not one to turn to
them. He had by then moved to the right of Gompers. He had by then begun his climb. His dream,
his moments of honest self-scrutiny and self-ap-
praisal (and he does occasionally have them, even
at the end of the trilogy, and even in the face of the
"accommodations" he makes as a calculating entrepreneur) are mere remnants, the stuff of life that
preoccupies sensitive novelists, interested in the

ironic distance that separates psychological energy
from the "actuality" that James Agee (in *Let Us
Now Praise Famous Men*) kept trying to describe:
the things we do—and do to each other—not because of, but regardless of the particular thoughts
we happen to have.[8]

Williams shrewdly places immediately after his
"psychological" chapter, "Night," a chapter utterly
and explicitly devoted to economic and political
matters. The title is "Inks, Presses and Personnel,"
and Joe is no longer a frog, even a lizard-like one.
Nor is he uncertain about what to do with himself.
He is a predator, hungry and on the hunt. He needs
ink in a hurry, for a business he is thoroughly intent
on setting up, no matter the effort of his former boss
and others to keep' him from doing so. When one of
the company officials he visits asks him where he
got his money, Joe is not embarrassed, or moved to a
personal, psychological "crisis": guilt and recrimi-
nation. Nor an existential crisis: the whys, ifs, and
buts that a day-time reverie or a night's dream can
prompt. "Money talks," he answers directly. He is
all business. He stares at the man he is talking to.
He is cynical, even crude. He is in a hurry. He
wants something and he will get it, period.

Such determination will, of course, affect a man's
home life. No matter how soft and gentle Joe
Stecher is with his wife and children, and no
matter how convinced Gurlie is that her social

and economic aspirations are, in fact, gestures of affection for her children, and understandable as such, Flossie senses the underlying tensions her parents are struggling with, and their consequent self-centeredness. There are, every day, all sorts of innocuous incidents, apparently of no great significance, which in fact exert a brutally decisive influence on the child, and which belie any number of her parents' dearly held illusions: we are giving our children everything, enjoy doing so, and in turn are appreciated for our altruistic love, and so on. For example, Flossie's doll is taken away: "That's too fine a thing for a child like that." Even an apple will suffice as an edifying occasion: "I want an apple!" Flossie exclaims, and Gurlie says, "No, no, no, no!" Then she explains: "Not now. We are going to save these. You'll get them later. We'll save them." And in case that isn't strong and specific enough: "I don't want her to have it. It will spoil her supper." At the very end of *In the Money*, it is Joe, not Gurlie, who is accused by his daughter Lottie and sister-in-law Olga of being a tease. He becomes competitive; they may have seen wonderful apple trees in the country, but there are plum trees right outside, part of their new suburban house, and they offer large, juicy fruit—better than any other. The children and their aunt know that he is fooling, but he is a little too serious; his dander is up: no one is going to win over him on any score.

Olga chastises him; so does his daughter. He defends himself: the children will "forget all about
it" in the morning. "I hope so," Olga says abruptly,
thereby indicating the seriousness of her objection
to his teasing. Then, as if to anticipate his annoyance, and, perhaps, go even further as a critical observer, she asks whether she might not best leave:
"You have no room for me here."

Williams makes no great production out of such
encounters; they are woven into the novel's fabric
so smoothly and unostentatiously that one hesitates to single them out for particular attention. But
they keep coming up, and they fit in with the
author's own analysis of what he intended when he
conceived and wrote his trilogy. The children, especially Flossie, whose birth marks, as well, the
birth of the three volumes, are mirrors of a kind;
they reflect the world around them, and help us see
what we otherwise might overlook: the driving insecurity of Gurlie, for instance, as an expression of
an all-encompassing egoism, which defies exact
explanation, and never really is brought under
effective control. Gurlie is not abrasive only when
the question of money comes up; nor is Joe tough
only with his business competitors. (He, too, becomes increasingly wrapped up in himself as he
makes his various business deals.) In the very first
chapter of *The Build-Up*, he author picks right up
with the theme he has been developing in the last

pages of *In the Money* — how a family's rise to social
prominence and financial success has an enormous,
yet quite subtle psychological impact on the way
parents get along with their children, and children
grow to think about themselves. At some point the
world of commerce and industry exerts its demands
on the very young. Children of the poor learn to expect little ahead for themselves. Children born to
those only marginally well-off may indeed hope for
more, but must learn early on that there is a price.
One has to save, be watchful, keep his or her guard
up. "Life is no picnic," I keep hearing from factory
workers; and their children hear the same words.
It is all very well for some of us to regard the remark as yet another cliché; for millions it is, rather,
a deeply felt statement of fact whose importance
simply must be conveyed to children — or else. On
the other hand, those same factory workers, like
Gurlie and Joe, don't sit down with their sons and
daughters in order to give them a sermon or two on
class and caste. In the course of living there are
many chances for the instruction of children; and
the lessons are learnt best when they are explicitly
tied to those seemingly innocuous issues; to wear
this or that; to use something now, or save it for a
later time; to enjoy this day or week, or to sacrifice
time now in the hope that later — always later, it
seems — there will be more, much more, to enjoy.

When that future time becomes the present, as

it does for those who aren't just "in" some money, but have arrived at a position for a "build-up," other psychological "adjustments" become necessary. Williams has a disarmingly simple way of introducing them, but he clearly knows what he wants us to know—even as he knows what Joe, Gurlie, and their children gradually come to know. He continues in *The Build-Up* to look at the social circumstances that confront the Stechers through the eyes of Flossie and Lottie—a new house, with upstairs and downstairs, or that peculiar silence and isolation that suburbs offer, with each family all too evidently on its own. The first chapters of *The Build-Up* show Flossie seven years old, rather than newborn; but the difficulties we learned about right at the start of *White Mule* persist in *The Build-Up*, and will never really go away. Flossie's father has done well in those seven years, and promises to do even better in the next seven. Flossie's mother has new tastes, ambitions, unfulfilled desires. And Flossie is, of course, their daughter; she has learned to be afraid of her mother, to rely upon her father for affection. She has also learned to be wary, self-protective, competitive; her father is fighting his way to the top, urged on by her mother, and she is going to be no slouch, either.

Slowly, as Williams promised in his essay "*White Mule* Versus Poetry," the last novel in the trilogy becomes taken up almost exclusively with

attentive and suggestive social observation; the
Stecher family, and especially Flossie, become part
of a particular society whose many and contradictory (and amusing and sad) facets a novelist wants
to examine. There are none of the noisy, abrupt but
psychologically penetrating encounters between
Gurlie and Joe that one finds repeatedly in *White
Mule*. They do squabble from time to time; but with
restraint, almost with tact and *politesse* — as if their
neighbors somehow are watching and listening.
And maybe that is what happens when people
rather quickly move across railroad tracks and
county lines or up one or another hill. (Gurlie is
obsessed with hills. She wants to have a view — not
only of the sky and the trees, however; she would
like, as well, to see a few rooftops.) The more one
has in the way of money to pay others, prestige in
relation to others, and respect from others, the more
those others become very much a part of one's
mind. The Gurlie of *White Mule* was her own person; she cared not what anyone said or felt — even
her mother and her husband. She defied conventional pieties, while at the same time reassuring
herself that in her very own ways she was living up
to them. No, she wasn't going to be a "good"
mother, or a quiet, accepting wife. She ignored her
neighbors, insulted those who wanted to help her,
scorned those she passed on the street or had to
(reluctantly) sit near in a park. When she did break

out of her stony, self-regarding shell, when she responded to people just a bit, one pictured her as a turtle, its head at last out, but not for long.

A few years later, however, Gurlie is quite another person, in certain respects. She is very much interested in the suburban community she now calls home. She goes to meetings. She wants to get her husband to come to them, but he is not so eager. She has her "charities." She keeps a careful eye on how her friends and neighbors live: what do they wear, how do they speak, where do they vacation? She also makes revisions in her thinking; once unashamedly out for herself and her immediate family, she becomes upon occasion in *The Build-Up* surprisingly interested in, of all people, the poor: "This is a good town, we're interested in our poor. When we find them in need we'll help them, and you can't do anything about it. I don't care who you are." The "you" is an Irish Catholic priest, Father Kelly. He had heard that one of his parishioners, a Mrs. O'Halloran, had been the beneficiary of the Poor Fund of Riverdale, and he was angered. The Church should take care of Her own, he believed. Who was Gurlie (she had become an "administrator" of the Fund, a charitable effort of Riverdale's suburban families) to be meddling in the lives of people so removed and different from herself?

But Gurlie was not about to cower before a vig-

orous, truculent priest. Her friends, yes, they knew
fear, or perhaps it was, in the clutch, indifference;
"the other women," we are told, "sensing the deli-
cacy of the situation, and being not a little scared,
had gladly let her take on the job." In contrast,
Williams tells us — and we are not quite sure if it is
the opinion of those "other women" or his own
authorial aside — that such a confrontation was
Gurlie's "meat." Moreover, it "gave her a chance
to show up the others, besides which she was a
really courageous woman." So it had come about
that Gurlie now championed the poor, and even
fought possessively over them. And doing so had
become "really courageous" — on the assumption,
one gathers, that determination on behalf of oneself is greed, but becomes courage when directed
to furtherance of the welfare of others. Williams is
not about to disagree with such an analysis; he
actively proposes it. But he makes sure, all the
while, that we not lose sight of the irony: Gurlie's
"meat" has always been blunt expression of
opinion. Her "meat" had had its effect; her husband
listened and did his best to oblige. Now she had
someone else to tell off; and now she was reaching
out to those whom she a few years earlier wanted
so desperately to leave behind in Manhattan's
slums.

We are brought within close view of *noblesse
oblige* — an ingredient of upper-middle-class life,

a way of announcing one's own successful arrival in the well-off suburbs. Gurlie will never stop being a fighter, but she most certainly will modify the ideological justification for her combativeness. She is quick to alert herself to the danger of becoming known as a *nouvelle arriviste*. She realizes that one must slowly shed oneself of the more explicit signs of acquisitiveness. Not that one by any means stops wanting things; stops insisting that X or Y are virtual necessities. But if a person is to be thought comfortably "in the money," quite on the way to being well-to-do, he or she has to demonstrate a degree of restraint, a certain casualness of manner with regard to property and possessions. What better way to prove one's own assured situation than to be solicitous toward others, and thereby have them as grateful sources of confirmation: we thank you for your charity, and it bothers us not at all — we have other things on our minds — if you let everyone in earshot know the vast difference between us. Meanwhile, of course, Gurlie keeps her eye out for the gestures and affirmations she *is* permitted — the discreet indications that she and her family have, as some put it today, definitely "made it."

Very important in such a scheme of things is education. Williams knew and described (in *The Build-Up*) how important many suburban families feel it to be that their children be kept to themselves at school—away, that is, from what a self-satisfied mother, as sure of herself as Gurlie, refers to as "many undesirable elements." Williams is brilliant at showing not only how social climbers go about their various activities, but who they can rely upon for assistance. In this instance it is school-teachers and their superintendents; they are quite willing to go along with the arrogant, snobbish demands of various suburban matrons—that a town's "better" children be segregated from its, again, "undesirable elements." But Flossie ends up with those "elements"; we are told that *somebody* had to be sacrificed." Now Gurlie and Joe have to face each other again. Joe's almost forgotten populist side reappears: fine, let the girl get to know children different from herself in various ways. Gurlie, as can be expected, won't go along with that kind of self-sacrificing idealism; but as she fights for Flossie's transfer to another classroom, she mouths egalitarian principles, which now and then do have a way of coming in handy. Addressing the superintendent, she insists that he is not the man in charge of only "one group of pupils." Then she broadens her charge: "Your salary is paid by the taxpayers to represent all of us. You have to treat us all equally. It is not fair if you choose one set. . . ." Whereupon the man interrupts. He is shocked that even the hint of being "unfair" would be directed at him.

It is a marvelous charade the two are conducting; the novelist has arranged it so that liberal pieties get shown for what they are: espoused passionately sometimes, dispensed without the slightest embarrassment, or sense of inconsistency, at other times. Gurlie is not being facetious when she demands equality; nor is the superintendent displaying mock incredulity when he wonders how she can possibly make the accusation she does. Dozens of social scientists have tried to fathom how suburban mothers and fathers can talk as they do about the prospect of their children receiving black classmates — that is, by invoking "justice," what is "right," what the Constitution, including the Bill of Rights, guarantees, and above all, what is "fair." Often such parents are called prejudiced, or "insecure," or suffering from the anxieties felt by marginally middle-class owners of small homes. Rarely do those of us who "study" such individuals try to understand how deeply convinced they are when they speak as they do, and how earnestly they struggle to make sense of the very contradictions we whose business it is to make "observations" keep on noticing. Williams is quite sure that both Gurlie and the self-righteous, clever superintendent did indeed mean what they said. If they were also hypocrites and if each was quite cunning, then that is perhaps the way it goes with the rest of us, including a good number of the best-educated

and politically best-intentioned, who also must
struggle with America's ambiguities as well as
their own "ambivalence."

Williams' purpose as a novelist requires as much
restraint as his characters possess. Even as they
have acquired a kind of exterior or social control
which actually runs deep and can be considered
quite automatic, if not, at the least, semi-conscious
(Gurlie and Joe are, again, far more "civilized" in
the private conversation of *The Build-Up*, even
when they argue), the man who created them,
through his narrative voice, is careful to watch *his*
step and avoid the temptations of suburban life: so
much to mock, ridicule, attack directly and harshly.
Gurlie holds her tongue when she confronts the
superintendent; gets across her disapproval, but
does not appear wild with rage, full of threats and
insults. With Joe, afterwards, she is indeed "furi-
ous," and warns him that she'll sooner take Flossie
out of school than submit to the superintendent's
will. But Williams ends the chapter quite abruptly —
as if to say that Gurlie quickly recovered her "cool,"
Joe quickly went back to his business concerns,
and naturally, Flossie did not forever stay with the
"wrong" schoolmates. The next chapter breezily
proceeds to yet another aspect of suburban life:
women's clubs and the celebration of holidays, in
this case, Valentine's Day.

It is not that we are denied a glimpse of the mean,

competitive, manipulative side of the suburb Riverdale, where the Stechers have both arrived and feel
in-between — having risen only so far, and being in
sight of so much further social territory to cross.
Williams' ear for ordinary conversation was not
confined to the northern New Jersey working-class
communities he both observed and served as a
physician. He can take a word or two, like "big-
shot," or "stuck-up," or "four-flusher," or "all
show," or "good-for-nothing," and use it or them as
the evocative centerpiece of a page, sometimes a
chapter: a means of reminding the reader who so-
and-so *was* and *is,* for all the airs or pretense that
he or she can manage. Joe notices with disdain the
people who are "all show," as he puts it; he refers
to their "society foolishness" — but he also goes on
making more and more, spending more and more,
and not incidentally, enjoying the life he is lead-
ing. That last aspect of his life, and of Gurlie's, too,
is crucial for Williams. He will not turn every plea-
surable moment into an occasion for scorn or parody.
He has consciously decided to balance his descriptions, his characterizations; we grow not only
increasingly familiar with the Stechers as we follow their history through the trilogy, but we understand them, and for all their limitations, feel close
to them — or so the author hopes.

This matter of the reader's distance, or lack of it,
as arranged, indeed sought, by the novelist, is

obvious consequence. The novelist's attitude not only affects ours, but determines more than the tone of his writing; content, as well, is affected. The suburbs enable families to forget the city, to ignore the brutal, forbidding slums and the mean, vicious, cut-throat rivalry of commercial life. Children are given wholesome, "clean" lives, and expressions like "how much did you *take?*" or "how much did you *clear?*," ingeniously used by Williams in situations which involve family conversation, are to an extent stripped of their crude implications. Only to an extent, one has to emphasize: suburbia is indeed a fantasy, a state of mind as much as a concrete, here-and-now condition — homes, yards, shopping plazas, community "fries" or "benefits," and almost endlessly on and on. But a fantasy lived out, a fantasy given the ongoing substance of bricks and mortar, is also part of "reality." A novelist can demolish that "reality," in order to expose the "real truth," his version of an "underlying reality," or he can say, as Williams does: yes, it happens, all this lust and contention and duplicity and vulgarity and sleaziness and determination and pleasant, joyful living and even genuine courage; I can only try to show as many sides of what I see going on as my gifts as a story-teller permit.

In *The Build-Up,* Joe's business dealings virtually disappear. Without in any way making a point of what he has done, Williams quite simply

allows Riverdale, and beyond it, the countryside of
New England and New York, the supremacy Joe
and Gurlie hoped for when they moved: a bit of
remove from the "system." In *White Mule*, Gurlie
nags Joe, and Joe, in turn, calculates what he has
to do, if he is to distinguish himself from millions
of others, who never for a moment have any financial independence. All during *In the Money* he
takes the steps he has come to realize as necessary—for him as well as his wife, because his mind
is fully capable of taking up where his wife's has
left off. (Gurlie never really told him what, specifically, to do—only do something, *anything*, that
would bring about the upward movement of the
Stechers.) In *The Build-Up*, Joe leaves for work, and
that is that. When he comes home he seems quite
willing to forget the office and content with the
maneuvers of his wife and her friends or neighbors:
who says what about whom; who has what position
in which charity drive, club, or activity. And, of
course, there are the children, in whose name so
many people of Riverdale have struggled, sacrificed,
and sometimes given themselves a hoist or two at
the expense of others, who get left behind in the
slums of New York City and elsewhere; in the name
of the future of those children, conversations are
held, purchases made, trips taken, land and summer houses bought, money put away in various
places. As for Gurlie, she becomes a restive but

complacent suburban housewife. She wants to live
in an even better neighborhood. She dreams of redemptive glory — her ancestral Norwegian home, in
all its past grandeur, real or imaginary, brought to
life through infusions of tainted but powerful American dollars. And finally, of course, she has understandable spells of sadness and bitterness, which
become, of all ironies, a new motive for materialist
acquisition: the privacy a large house with plenty
of surrounding land can afford a lonely woman and
her husband, who have lost their only son.

What is one to say about Paul Stecher, the third
child of Gurlie and Joe, who appears in *The Build-
Up*, and soon enough dies of an accidental self-
inflicted gunshot wound? Williams not only moves
his characters more rapidly through time in this
last novel, but engages them more consistently with
others outside the family — another contribution of
suburban life: lawns connect with other lawns, and
one has to have an audience for one's achievements
and, in turn, be a witness to those of others. Even
though we know full well what the birth of a son
means to Gurlie and Joe, there is remarkably little
given us about the boy himself; his childhood is
virtually ignored, amid the description of the
family's various suburban encounters. We are told
that Paul was a marvelous child, handsome, intelligent, and resourceful, but we are offered little
evidence to sustain the assertion — not words or

actions of the boy, not responses to him or reflections upon his nature on the part of his parents.
His presence seems to be yet another indication of
fate's generosity: there is nothing, at least for a
while, that is to be denied Gurlie, so in need of
fulfillment, and Joe, ever anxious to prove that it all
pays off—the combination of hard work and self-
proclaimed modesty, lightly seasoned with that
business guile which any number of deacons of
various churches claim even Christ Himself sanc-
tioned (in the reference to "serpents and doves").
But the countryside, the rolling hills and inviting
valleys which Gurlie had so frequently regarded as
nurturing and liberating, turned out to be the scene
of an awful disaster; and she herself thereafter is
quick to recognize her own past mistake. After her
son's death near the Stecher country home, she
wants no more part of the place. But she cannot at
that late moment in her life become another person. Nor can Joe. They can see the country for what
it is, no haven, no acreage belonging to a New Jerusalem. They cannot, though, let go of everything.
What is left, of course, is a chance for a yet larger
home in a more exclusive neighborhood.

What is left is America, and all it offers to certain
people—who, while their energy and will last, can
shake their fists at the world when it seems to be
unfriendly, and rush onward and upward: not in
search of themselves, not in pursuit of some expla-

nation of things, some philosophical viewpoint, some evidence of God's grace or even their fellow man's approval or sanction, but quite simply, and without ending: more. That is the point at which Dr. Williams has chosen to conclude his trilogy — with the Stechers proceeding in full haste and without the slightest inclination for pause upon their further "build-up." Now, nearly a quarter of a century after the trilogy was completed, given the state of this nation — its air contaminated, its streams, the Passaic certainly foremost among them, badly polluted, its land in so many places torn apart and ravaged, its economy all hyped up and depressed at the same time — who is to say that there is anything quaint or out-of-date about the Stechers and the place where their creator Dr. William Carlos Williams chose to leave them?

NOTES

PART ONE

1. *Paterson* has, in fact, received a good deal of critical attention, as has Williams' other poetry. Joel Conarroe has devoted
a whole book to the five sections of Williams' long poem:
Paterson: Language and Landscape (Philadelphia, 1970). His
book provides a valuable introduction to the various analytical
essays that poets and literary critics have written. Especially
valuable collections of those essays, including efforts to come
to terms with Williams' other poetry, are *William Carlos
Williams: A Collection of Critical Essays,* edited by J. Hillis
Miller (Englewood Cliffs, New Jersey, 1966), and *Profile of
William Carlos Williams,* compiled by Jerome Mazzaro (Columbus, Ohio, 1971). An interesting new book on Williams'
poetry—and through it, on the nature of language, considered
as both a psychological and philosophical "problem"—is
Joseph Riddel's *The Inverted Bell: Modernism and the Coun-
ter-poetics of William Carlos Williams* (Baton Rouge, 1974). An
issue of *The Journal of Modern Literature* was devoted to Dr.
Williams' work: May, 1971. In it one finds an especially original examination of *Paterson,* Sister Bernetta Quinn's *"Paterson:
Landscape and Dream."* In the Penguin critical anthology
devoted to Williams, edited by Charles Tomlinson (London,
1972) one finds a whole section with the title: "The Debate on
Paterson." Robert Lowell and Randall Jarrell both contribute
to the "debate," not exactly on the same side—though Jarrell,
for all his inclination to be skeptical of or sharp with Williams,
does indeed at times respond favorably to *Paterson.* But less
well known and wonderfully stimulating is Edward Dahlberg's
piece: "Word-Sick and Peace-Crazy," a worthy moment of
resonance, one can call it, both empathic and suspicious, to
Williams' own poetry. Mr. Tomlinson also has a fine essay on
Williams' poetry, and especially, *Paterson,* in *Encounter,*
November, 1967.

Paterson is, of course, examined at substantial length in six books which combine in varying degrees biographical narrative with broad interpretation of a prolific writer's lifework. Vivienne Koch's *William Carlos Williams* (Norfolk, Connecticut, 1950) offered the first book-length survey of Dr. Williams. *Paterson* was being written when Ms. Koch's book appeared; she can, therefore, examine only Book One and Book Two, but does so with grace and clarity. John Malcom Brinnin's brief sketch, one of the University of Minnesota series on American writers (Minneapolis, 1963), is helpful and suggestive. One gets a nice sense of comparison between *Paterson* and other, comparable yet different, long poems: Eliot's *Four Quartets* and Hart Crane's *The Bridge*. A longer and quite helpful study of all of Williams' poetry with, of course, an extended discussion of *Paterson* is to be found in Alan Ostrom's *The Poetic World of William Carlos Williams* (Carbondale, Illinois, 1966). James Guimond approaches *Paterson,* and indeed all of Williams' writing, with a keen interest in the personal and social forces at work in a particular poet and novelist—Williams as a second-generation American who was virtually possessed by a search for the essence, if such there is, of this nation's culture: *The Art of William Carlos Williams: A Discovery and Possession of America* (Urbana, Illinois, 1968). In the same year Thomas R. Whitaker published his quite finely written and suggestive *William Carlos Williams* (New York); it is, to be sure, a relatively brief exegetical book, but the author has a good sense, I believe, of what Williams was about when he attempted *Paterson*—and there is an especially pointed section on his prose. James E. Breslin's book *William Carlos Williams: An American Artist* (New York, 1970) in a somewhat similar vein makes an effort to "place" the author who himself tried so stubbornly to "place," with respect to language, time, region, so many Americans. A remark like "Williams spent some thirty years of living and writing in preparation for *Paterson*," though not in and of itself brilliant, sets the stage for a quite refreshing kind of good sense; we are spared the microscopic criticism that separates an author's words from his life, but also spared the extravagances and arrogance of an excessively "psychological" approach to the work of a given artist. Also of substance and intellectual richness—but not arid—is Mike Weaver's *William Carlos Williams: The American Background* (Cambridge, England, 1971).

Even books devoted to Williams' prose or his early poetry cannot escape *Paterson;* for instance, Bram Dijkstra's *The Hieroglyphics of a New Speech; Cubism, Stieglitz, and The Early Poetry of William Carlos Williams* (Princeton, 1969), or Linda W. Wagner's scholarly *The Prose of William Carlos Williams* (Middletown, Connecticut, 1970). (*Paterson,* of course, has its fair share of prose—a dramatic and controversial device Williams uses from time to time in the poem.) Although John Engels' *Guide to William Carlos Williams* (Columbus, Ohio, 1969) is short and unpretentious, intended as an introductory essay, it provides some lively observations on Williams' poetry, including *Paterson.* In a special class, obviously, is *The Literary Heritage of New Jersey,* (New York and Princeton, 1964), the joint effort of Lawrence Holland, Nathanial Burt, and A. Walton Litz. I believe Williams would have loved finding himself given a context of sorts: New Jersey as a state with a quite special historical and literary tradition. And finally, there is all that Dr. Williams himself wrote about his poetry: one need not list the articles, so many of them; one need only refer the reader to, and be enormously grateful for, Emily Mitchell Wallace's work of precision, discrimination, and love: *A Bibliography of William Carlos Williams,* (Middletown, Connecticut, 1968).

2. See his own account of his life, an autobiography that reads like a solid, inviting story: *The Autobiography of William Carlos Williams,* (New York, 1951).

3. An excellent discussion of the novels mentioned, and many others, is provided in Elwood P. Lawrence's *The Immigrant in American Fiction*—which, alas, is not published, but is available from the library of Western Reserve University in Cleveland, Ohio, as a thesis submitted in 1943 for the Degree of Doctor of Philosophy in the Department of English. There is a first-rate bibliography in Dr. Lawrence's manuscript. Also of interest, in this regard, is Blanche Gelfant's *The American City Novel,* (Norman, Oklahoma, 1954); and Barbara Miller Solomon's excellent *Ancestors and Immigrants: A Changing New England Tradition,* (Chicago, 1956).

4. See Pupin's *From Immigrant to Inventor* (New York, 1923); Bok's *The Americanization of Edward Bok* (New York, 1920) and his less well known, and more self-congratulatory and chauvinistic *Twice Thirty Years* (New York, 1925); and finally, the old shrewd Scotsman Carnegie's *Autobiography* (Boston, 1920).

5. Williams could become querulous, if not outraged by words — "goddam words," he once said, when confiding his earliest ambition: to be an artist, to put on canvas what he felt, leaving the reader to make of the effort what he or she could or would. He would no doubt have responded warmly and sadly (for its content) to George Tice's patient, thorough, and strong collection of photographs, which silently takes the measure of today's Paterson — and does so with no ideological axe to grind: *Paterson* (New Brunswick, New Jersey, 1972). As one goes through Tice's photographs the Passaic stories and the long poem *Paterson* keep coming to mind, page after page.

PART TWO

1. I do think Melanie Klein would find Williams' portrait of an infant's life rather satisfying. Unfortunately, she insisted upon making her view of the infant's first months "scientific": "stages," "positions" — in sum, efforts to classify the continuity and flux of days, weeks, months. And as she *formulated* her hunches, and applied to them bulky and portentous words ("paranoid position") an air of unreality comes over the "subject-matter." One wants to ask, as Anna Freud has, for more "direct observation," and less theoretical elaboration. I have discussed this matter at some length in a previous book, *The Mind's Fate* (Boston, 1975). In any event, Williams supplies what Miss Freud urges, the clinician's plain, straightforward impressions, which lead one *toward,* it can be argued, some of Miss Klein's way of looking at infants, but *only* toward. We cannot, so far, know, only surmise, what "thoughts" infants have in those rather tumultuous (the growth, the rapid, feverish growth!) first months of life. See Melanie Klein, *The Psychoanalysis of Children* (London, 1932) and in contrast, Anna

Freud's *Collected Writings*, especially Volume IV (New York, 1968).

2. If I am a little cranky here with Ms. Koch, I want to register my enthusiasm for her approach both to the Passaic stories and the Stecher trilogy. Other valuable treatments of the prose discussed here are to be found in the books by Wagner, Weaver, Breslin, and Whitaker cited in the first note of Part One. Of considerable interest, still, are some of the reviews which came out when *White Mule* appeared in 1937: Babette Deutsch's review in the *New York Sun;* Willard Maas' fine essay in the *New York Herald Tribune,* and Alfred Kazin's, one of his very best, in the *New York Times.* Philip Rahv's essay on *White Mule* in the *Nation,* and essay on the Passaic stories which appeared in *Image and Idea* (Norfolk, Connecticut, 1957), and originally in *Partisan Review,* are pungent, intelligent, lyrical responses to Dr. Williams' writing. Van Wyck Brooks had a delightful essay published in *Harper's,* June, 1961; it deals sensitively with Williams' short stories. And, of course, there is Williams' own *"White Mule* Versus Poetry," which appeared in *The Writer,* August, 1937 — a brief spirited, confiding, effort to show that distinctions like "prose" and "poetry" in one writer's mind, at least, were not all that distinct and fixed.

3. Erik Erikson's work is, of course, an exception. Simone Weil's *The Need For Roots* (New York 1952) offers the most thoughtful analysis I know — from a moral philosopher, not a child psychiatrist — of the meaning work has for all families.

4. See, especially, Breslin's chapter "The Fiction of a Doctor" in *William Carlos Williams: An American Artist.*

5. I leap from the Stechers to that incurable American romantic adventurer, Richard Halliburton, whose *Royal Road to Romance* (New York, 1925) I happen to remember rather vividly from my childhood, because Williams was quite familiar with the romantic nonsense Joe and Gurlie firmly rejected, however swift their "rise." Williams was considered by some poets and critics a romantic himself, but he never allowed any aesthetic romanticism toward which he may have been drawn to affect his rather consistently realistic, sardonic, and even gloomy view of America's social and economic system.

PART THREE

1. See Michael Hoffman's *The Development of Abstractionism in the Writings of Gertrude Stein* (Philadelphia, 1965).

2. There is an informative and humorous discussion by Williams of his encounter with Gertrude Stein in the *Autobiography*. Writers like Weaver and Breslin, and John Malcom Brinnin (who is especially knowing about both Williams and Stein) remark often on the shared concerns the two had for identifying, as best they could, what it meant to be an American. See Brinnin's *The Third Rose: Gertrude Stein and Her World* (Boston, 1959).

3. See, in example, Joseph Blotner's *The Modern American Political Novel, 1900–1960* (Austin, Texas, 1966); or Walter Ridout's *The Radical Novel in the United States, 1900–1954* (Cambridge, Massachusetts, 1956). Good efforts to come to terms with Dos Passos, and especially *U.S.A.*, are Melvin Landsberg's *Dos Passos' Path to U.S.A.* (Boulder, Colorado, 1972) and John Brantley's, *The Fiction of John Dos Passos* (Hague, The Netherlands, 1968). The latter offers an especially trenchant evaluation of Dos Passos as a particular kind of American radical writer (for a time, at least). And of real distinction is Kenneth Lynn's essay "The Achievement of John Dos Passos" in his *Visions of America* (Westport, Connecticut, 1973).

4. See C. Vann Woodword's historical (and unselfconsciously psychological) portrait: *Tom Watson: Agrarian Rebel* (New York, 1963).

5. His book was published in 1973 (New York); it is a gem of social history and offers much illumination to what Williams was struggling with. Equally helpful is Kenneth Lynn's *The Dream of Success* (Boston, 1955).

6. Williams himself discusses his complicated attitude toward Whitman in "An Approach to the Poem," which appears in *English Institute Essays: 1947* (New York, 1965). (Originally published by Columbia University Press, New York, 1948.)

7. See, again, her *The Need For Roots*.

8. I try to discuss Agee's view of "human actuality" in "James Agee's 'Famous Men' Seen Again," in *Harvard Advocate*, February 1972; also in the book *Irony in the Mind's Life*, Charlottesville, 1974.

About the Author

Robert Coles was born in Boston in 1929, received his A.B. degree from Harvard College in 1950, and his medical degree from the College of Physicians and Surgeons at Columbia University in 1954. His internship was at the University of Chicago Clinics, his psychiatric residencies at Massachusetts General Hospital and McLean Hospital, and his residency in child psychiatry at the Children's Hospital in Boston. For over fifteen years he has been studying and working with the medical and psychological problems of a wide variety of American children: black and white children of the South; migrant and sharecropper children; Appalachian children; ghetto children in Northern cities; Indian, Chicano, and Eskimo children of the West; and children of the working class and of suburbia.

Dr. Coles's literary accomplishments have been as distinguished as his medical career. To date, he is the author of 24 books and some 500 essays, articles, and reviews. These have ranged from professional articles for medical journals to essays and literary criticism for a variety of publications, such as *The New Yorker, The Atlantic Monthly, Daedalus,* and *The New York Review of Books.* He is a contributing editor of *The New Republic, The American Scholar,* and *American Poetry Review.* In 1973 he received the Pulitzer Prize for *Migrants, Sharecroppers and Mountaineers* and *The South Goes North* (Volumes II and III of his series, *Children of Crisis*).